THE
HOLISTIC YOU

THE HOLISTIC YOU: WORKBOOK

Integrating Your Family, Finances, Faith, Friendships, and Fitness

RABBI DANIEL LAPIN
AND
SUSAN LAPIN

WILEY

Published by John Wiley & Sons, Inc., Hoboken, New Jersey.
Published simultaneously in Canada.

For general information on our other products and services or for technical support, please contact our
Customer Care Department within the United States at (800) 762-2974, outside the United States at (317)
572-3993 or fax (317) 572-4002.

Wiley also publishes its books in a variety of electronic formats. Some content that appears in print may not
be available in electronic formats. For more information about Wiley products, visit our web site at www.wiley
.com.

Library of Congress Cataloging-in-Publication Data is Available:

ISBN 9781394163496 (Paperback)
ISBN 9781394163533 (ePDF)
ISBN 9781394163526 (ePUB)

Cover Design and Image: Wiley

SKY10053159_081423

We humbly dedicate this book to our extraordinary children:

Rebecca and Max Masinter
Rena and Yoni Baron
Rachelle and Zev Stern
Ari and Menucha Lapin
Ruthie and Asher Abraham
Miriam and Anshel Kaplan
Tamara and David Sasson

With limitless admiration for what you have all become
and
with boundless appreciation for all you have done

Contents

Preface

We are not big fans of television. Nonetheless, on a trip once, we arrived in our hotel room to see the ubiquitous large-screen television on the wall. It was on but set on mute, so the tantalizing bright and fast-moving scenes were silent. Yet, no matter where we searched, all the usual places and others, we found no controller for the television. I (RDL) felt an almost irresistible compulsion to call the front desk and request a remote control for the television. Finally, I found the power switch on the bottom of the screen and turned it off. We laughed at how urgently I wanted to be able to control that television. Had it been off when we walked in, or had there been no television, I don't think it would have bothered me.

For someone utterly oblivious of the subconscious, those subtle but influential meanderings of the mind, not being able to control one's mind doesn't much matter. However, for those aware of their souls, it becomes important to be able to interact with those involuntary and unquantifiable parts of their beings.

But how does one shape one's beliefs? How does one generate optimism, sculpt one's outlook, and force happiness to well up in one's soul? After all, whether we are looking at the nervous young man staring, trying to summon up the courage to approach a pretty girl and ask her out on a date; the soldier in combat weighing up the risks and rewards of a potentially dangerous operation; or the young woman nervous before delivering a speech, believing in success makes the actions more likely to be undertaken and confers better chances of satisfactory outcomes.

That is what this book is about. It introduces you, the reader, to the actions and exercises that give you the remote control for your soul.

Think of the many little daily routines that we perform almost on autopilot. We brush our teeth without consciously deciding on exactly how much tooth-paste to use each morning. It is just as well that we don't have to expend brain energy on determining each little step toward our daily oral hygiene. Buttering our toast or any other eating routine also becomes what we call second nature. We do it without consciously thinking through the steps as we might do, say, when navigating our way to a never-before visited destination. As a matter of fact, shortly after relocating to our new home, I (SL) was driving home and suddenly found myself parked in front of our old home, the one we had vacated about a week earlier. That's right; I had been almost on autopilot, and my muscle-memory and subconscious mind had me do once again what I had done every day for a decade.

There are many times when we wish to take control of our subconscious, many times when we would love to hold the remote control for our souls in our hands.

Here is a story I (RDL) often tell audiences at my personal appearances. Imag-ine I am at the airport on my way to give a speech in one of those sad cities that possess what is euphemistically known as a bad part of town. What that means is a neighborhood so rife with crime that for ordinary tourists to venture there is tantamount to an invitation to be robbed. Forewarned is forearmed, so I diligently make my way to the airport bookstore and purchase myself a paperback copy of *Self-Defense in Ten Easy Lessons,* which I subsequently glance at during my flight. Later that night, I confidently venture out for an after-dinner stroll. With my copy of *Self-Defense in Ten Easy Lessons* safely stashed in my jacket pocket, I sally forth into the darkness.

Not surprisingly, I am soon startled by an arm around my neck from behind and the unpleasant sensation of something hard and metallic jabbing me in the ribs. A rather harsh sounding but unseen voice informs me that now would be a very good time to hand over my wallet and my watch if I retain any hope of continuing my walk. Nothing doing, think I. That informative volume nestled in my jacket pocket is my insurance policy. In fact, from my brief airborne perusal I recall that armed attacks from the rear were covered in Chapter 7.

"Just a moment," I politely react. "Ease up with that gun, would you? I need to get out my self-defense book and review exactly how to deal with your unprovoked interruption of my pleasant evening." My impatient assailant sounds even more irritated as he states that time is running out for the conclusion of our transaction, and furthermore, even if he allowed me to carefully read my entire book, it would in no way change the outcome of our little encounter.

And you know what? My imaginary mugger is absolutely correct. There was only one effective way to have prepared for our little property-transferring rendezvous, and putting a book in my pocket was not that way. What I should have done was to attend many sessions at the martial arts gym with a good unarmed combat teacher who would have repeatedly drilled me on each maneuver until it became, yes, second nature. My teacher would have helped me overcome my natural learned instinct not to hurt people. That way, the very instant that hostile arm snaked around my neck, every muscle in my body would have convulsed unthinkingly, and between my heel stomping down on his instep and my elbow connecting violently with his throat, the threat would have been averted before my conscious mind even realized what was happening. I should have reprogramed my soul. I should have re-scripted my spiritual schematic. But I didn't do so, and therefore on that fateful (but imaginary) evening, I would feel lucky to lose only my wallet and watch.

The sales professional who exudes a friendly, calm confidence enjoys a considerable advantage over her nervous and desperate colleague. The sprinter crouched on his starting blocks who radiates assurance of his soon-to-be-seen win, just as Usain Bolt did less than 10 seconds before he won the 100-meter race at the London Olympics in 2012, is more likely to win.

Almost every one of the dozens of instances during each day, when busy people are confronted by a decision that needs to be made, share a strategic factor. Most of those decisions need to be made quickly. One does not always have time for careful and cautious deliberation. Just as in self-defense, the body will only react quickly if it has been trained. A timely response to a child's inquiry, a business proposal, or a suggested social engagement, even if it is only a cheerful request to defer the decision, will reflect the spiritual matrices that have been set in place.

The anxious parent whose spiritual schematic is complete and integrated is more likely to make the right child-raising decision. A substantial advantage in every area of life is enjoyed by the individual who succeeds in not only knowing what to do but who also succeeds in transferring that knowledge from the brain to the heart, from the matter to the mind, from the body to the soul.

In the eight chapters that follow, we are going to help you sculpt your soul. Moreover, we shall equip you with that elusive, but oh so important, remote control for your soul.

Onward and upward,
Rabbi Daniel and Susan Lapin

Acknowledgements

One reason it can be hard to teach a toddler to say "thank you" is because acknowledging gratitude is like declaring a dependency. In the Lord's language, Hebrew, the word for expressing gratitude is the same as the word for confessing. "Thank you" means that I confess I needed you and I needed and value what you have done for me. For little people, it can be hard to acknowledge a need for others.

We, on the other hand, joyfully acknowledge our dependency upon so many others and our delight at the privilege of collaborating with them on this book. Our family deserves much gratitude for so often having had to yield to the book's priority. Many is the family occasion that we missed or for which we arrived late on account of our dedication to the book. They understand our unquenchable desire to make ancient Jewish wisdom accessible to as many people as possible and uncomplainingly make allowances for it.

Kevin Harreld at Wiley is as much a parent of this book as are we. Without his vision, encouragement, and guidance it simply would never have come to life. We appreciate him greatly. Kevin's amazing colleagues at Wiley shepherded us toward the finish line. You would not be holding this book in your hands without the steady stream of directives and patient professionalism of Susan Cerra and her team.

Our editor, Sheryl Nelson, has known us for years and still agreed to undertake the task of polishing our torrents of verbal enthusiasm into this now very readable book. A great editor doesn't just change; a great editor improves, and this Sheryl certainly did.

Emma Fialkoff, an accomplished author in her own right, heads our production team and has shared many late night hours with us as we struggled with one or another aspect of the book's architecture. We recognize that we are not the easiest of writers to work with, and she deserves much credit not only for what she did but for how she did it.

There would have been no chance of our having been able to concentrate for such extensive periods on this book exclusively unless we felt confident that our office would continue to run smoothly and effectively. That it did so is due to three remarkable women who are not only accomplished professionals but who have also become cherished friends. Crystol Garrison could easily be managing any large multinational corporation. That she has instead chosen to be the crucial lynchpin of our organization for so many years fills us with wonder and appreciation. We doubt that we could manage without her because in addition to all she accomplishes, she also brings out the best in us. Jessica Solberg Black is the personification of competence. Those words are often used to describe a soulless bureaucrat, but Jessica could hardly be more different. She is not only startlingly creative but successfully stimulates similar creativity among her team members. Ellen Joyce Garcia is the calm and experienced engineer deep down in the engine room of our ship. She keeps the machinery throbbing with purpose and power as our enterprise plows through the oceans and is a pleasure to work with.

Dina Bengio is our truly remarkable personal assistant who uncomplainingly makes problems vanish and frustrations evaporate. We are still trying to discover areas in which she possesses less than extraordinary experience and ability.

We close this altogether inadequate attempt at expressing our gratitude with a great big thank you to God Almighty without whom we doubt that we would have found one another and without whom nothing our marriage has achieved would have come to pass.

Rabbi Daniel & Susan Lapin
Maryland, 2023

About the Authors

For nearly two decades, Rabbi Daniel Lapin and his wife, Susan, led the Southern California congregation they planted and where they met and married. After counseling crowds of young people through career crises, dating dilemmas, and marriage mysteries by applying ancient Jewish wisdom to solve contemporary problems, word of their work began spreading beyond their own community into both Jewish and Christian circles. Their seven best-selling books, daily television show, weekly podcast, and the resources they create make their inviting, Bible-based approach to life's challenges accessible to people of every background. They are well-known speakers for Jewish, Christian, and business groups in the United Kingdom, Switzerland, South Africa, Ghana, Nigeria, Korea, China, and throughout North America.

While Susan grew up in New York, Rabbi Daniel was born and spent his early childhood in South Africa. His parents, the distinguished Rabbi and Mrs. A. H. Lapin, dispatched him to England and Israel even before he turned 13 to immerse him in Scripture. Though not a particularly studious young man to start with, he did eventually find himself intensely intrigued by the Bible, economics, physics, and mathematics, which he subsequently taught at Yeshiva College. As he puts it, "These disciplines explain how the world *really* works."

Rabbi Daniel and Susan Lapin have been blessed with seven children whom they greatly admire and who are now building their own young families. The Lapin children were homeschooled on Mercer Island, Washington, and the family enjoyed annual holidays boating off the coast of British Columbia. Several of the Lapin children joined their parents on an exciting Pacific Ocean crossing in their own sailboat, and some are now homeschooling Lapin grandchildren. The Lapins recently relocated to Maryland, where they live in one of the most vibrant Jewish communities in the United States.

Introduction

Welcome. This workbook is a companion to our book *The Holistic You: Integrating Your Family, Finances, Faith, Friendships, and Fitness.* *The Holistic You* provides you with a framework for thinking about your life in terms of a 5F system: Family, Faith, Friendship, Finance, and Fitness. In the book, we demonstrated the many ways in which these pillars interact within our lives, with the goal of inspiring you to implement the crosslinks between these areas in your own life and learning how to weld your life holistically rather than fragmenting your life.

This book is designed to carry you through an introspective journey that helps you to cultivate and strengthen each of your own 5Fs and take advantage of their interconnectedness. Reading *The Holistic You* will put you on the road to exciting transformation, and working through the activities in this guide will help you implement these powerful principles.

A great ocean liner changing course needs to do so smoothly, gradually, and firmly. Lurching from side to side at great speed doesn't work. In a similar way, changing course in your life should be done in discrete and fluid steps. The more thought and consistent effort you put into the exercises in this workbook, the more you will feel your course changing.

Before we begin, take a moment to reflect:

1. From 1–5, with 1 being *completely comfortable* and 5 being *unbearably painful,* rate how much dissonance you feel there is between goals and visions you have nurtured at different times and what you see as your current reality for each of your 5Fs

Family:	1	2	3	4	5
Faith:	1	2	3	4	5
Finance:	1	2	3	4	5
Fitness:	1	2	3	4	5
Friendship:	1	2	3	4	5

2. What are your three challenges that generate most dissonance?

_____

_____

_____

The Purpose of This Workbook

Many books have been written to teach readers how to achieve success by focusing on one of the five pillars that we integrate in *The Holistic You*. Countless books talk about how to make money, how to have good relationships, how to have faith, and so on. Our goal is to correct the misconception that these areas can be improved separately (though having books dedicated to each one is by no means improper) and reveal the ways that each of the five pillars of a healthy life support and influence each other.

Without an understanding of this holistic interaction, we are all at risk. Have you ever met someone who deferred marriage because he wanted to focus exclusively on his career—and yet continued not to succeed professionally and didn't get married either?! Or someone who worked ceaselessly to lose weight but never succeeded until she addressed the emotional trauma that was preventing her from moving forward?

When we learn to harness the power of our own holistic system, we avoid a tunnel-vision focus on one aspect of life that can otherwise consume all our energies. Very often, the solutions to a problem in one area of life may lie in another area of life entirely. The more we understand how the five pillars interact, the more we will develop the ability to perceive these possible links and utilize them to our benefit.

Overview of This Guide

In the following pages, we will start by confronting the myths of happiness that our culture beams at us and suggesting that many of us have been accepting faulty information from flawed sources of authority. We will then explore what sources of data we want to turn to in our lives. Much of how our lives evolve depends on who and what we allow to influence us.

Here is a reminder of how we define the 5Fs. We will then explore them in more depth:

1. **Family:** These are the relationships we have with parents, siblings, spouses, children, and other blood relatives or relatives through marriage. From another perspective, we speak of family as the relationships that result from sexual connection. When we share a joyful multigenerational family gathering, as awkward as it might be to think about, we sometimes forget that the only reason we are there with uncles and aunts and cousins is because many years ago, Grandpa and Grandma's eyes met, they formed a bond and later found ecstasy in one another's arms.

2. **Finance:** This covers relationships with our possessions and with our money in all its forms. It includes human connections that revolve around money. Employers, employees, customers and clients, work associates, professional associations, and vendors all fall under this pillar.

3. **Friendship:** This includes friends or people we connect with through shared interests like hobbies or sports, local events, or our children's education. Political, civic, and social groups with which we associate and charity organizations in which we participate also fall under this category. Likewise, the experience of "community" that many people feel through association with a religion is part of the friendship pillar. Most relationships with people who are linked to us neither through family nor money fall into this category.

4. **Faith:** Faith refers to our relationship with things that cannot be measured in a laboratory. Faith may be a commitment to integrity, say, or the love and esteem of others that we feel. Whatever beliefs play a role in our lives or set of values that governs our decision-making fall under the Faith heading as does, obviously, a relationship with God.

5. Fitness: This pillar refers to everything having to do with our bodies—our anatomy, physiology, and biology. Fitness covers our health and how we maintain it. How we eat, breathe, excrete, drink, make love, and eventually die are all covered in detail in ancient Jewish wisdom.

As we explore the 5Fs, we will uncover many of the ways that they interact with one another in our lives with all their complexities.

How to Use This Workbook

This guide is meant to be used in connection with the book *The Holistic You*. We strongly recommend that you read *The Holistic You* before you work on this guide.

We recommend working through the book from beginning to end as the ideal way to complete it. Because the topics are heavily interrelated, you may find that an exercise in the chapter about, say, fitness, will answer questions you've had about finance and vice versa. Additionally, some of the early exercises are important for laying the foundation for engaging in this process. For this reason, a non-sequential completion of the exercises will not be as beneficial as completing them in the order that they appear.

Question Types

This book contains several different types of questions that should be answered in different ways.

Some questions are simple self-reflection questions that ask you to look at your own life and experiences. Others ask that you examine prevailing notions and beliefs in our society and determine whether those beliefs are worth adopting. Still other questions ask you to think about the nature of life and about how the five pillars interact. We hope that many will prompt you to make resolutions and spark growth.

We would like to highlight one difference between an exercise called "sentence stems" and another one called "thought exercises" because they require a very different approach.

Sentence Stems: A sentence stem is where we provide you with the beginning of a sentence and invite you to fill out the remainder of the sentence in the white space. The way to complete sentence stems is to fill in the blank as quickly and instinctively as possible. These are not exercises that demand deep thought but are rather meant to help you connect with the things you already think and believe, though perhaps beneath your conscious awareness. By completing the sentence quickly, you ensure that you don't overthink the exercise, which can interfere with you accessing your current subconscious beliefs.

Thought Exercises and Experiments: Another exercise that you will find in this book is the thought exercise. In some ways, the thought exercise is the opposite of the sentence stem in that we advise you to think deeply about the answers. The goal is not to reveal what current beliefs lurk just beneath the surface of your conscious awareness, but rather to think deeply about things that you have perhaps given very little thought to before.

We encourage you to work through this book gradually, allowing each exercise to sink in. You may be able to complete some exercises in one sitting or you may find that the questions stay with you for days or longer. That is okay.

In fact, we encourage you to continue to mull over the more difficult questions when you are driving, cooking, or taking a walk. The point is to bring your active brain power into the equation and really put both your conscious and subconscious minds to work.

A Word of Warning

Before we dive into this workbook, we would like to give a word of warning. Though some of the questions asked in the coming pages will provoke no emotional dissonance, others will surprise you with the intensity of feeling they generate within you. They may require deep thought and reflection, and they may ask you to confront aspects of your life that are uncomfortable for you. It is possible that every molecule of your being will rebel at allowing your thoughts to go in certain directions. After all, our bodies are designed to try to avoid pain. But as the famous body builder of the last century, Charles Atlas, used to say, no pain, no gain.

Some ideas may challenge deeply held beliefs. Others may force you to ponder things that have no easy answer or that take extensive time to answer. The process of knowing ourselves and of being willing to see what is true and what is false is not an easy one. But it is well worth it.

Before entering the land of Israel, God directed the Israelites to *be strong and resolute*. Even a task for which they were destined required courage and resolve to complete. Likewise, as we look to take control of our lives, a task for which we are all unquestionably destined, we must be strong and resolute and muster the courage to face difficult questions with honesty and openness. If we can do this, we can achieve something truly beautiful: a holistic, balanced, and meaningful life.

Chapter 1

Meeting the Five Fs

A full and active life has so many aspects. We are sure you can think of many things that contribute to a full life. For instance, how about fun? Marriage? Children? Pets? Hobbies? Friends? Livelihood? Travel? Appreciation of art and music? Any others?

Now we ask you to carefully contemplate whether some of those qualities and activities just mentioned are intrinsic to a good life while others are auxiliary rather than indispensable.

It might help if you give some thought to the definition and meaning of concepts like fun, art appreciation, and others.

The premise of this book is that five areas are vital to a complete and successful life. We call them the 5Fs, and they consist of Family, Faith, Friendship, Finance, and Fitness. Areas such as pets and travel certainly appeal to people, but they belong in an already built life. Think in terms of whether an aspect of life is foundational, like the reinforced concrete basis for a building, or whether it is more like the carpet choice that will later be made. Not only are the 5Fs necessary, but they all interact with and affect each of the other areas.

This workbook will be most useful when used as an adjunct to our book *The Holistic You*. Some of the exercises might be interesting on their own, but many of the definitions and purposes of the exercises will only be clear once you have read the book.

Start training your instincts to think in terms of systems rather than discrete elements. You wouldn't take a medicine to heal your skin if it put the rest of your bodily health in danger. Likewise, you wouldn't drive a car with a working engine but no brakes.

When dealing with a system, we are working with a group of components that must all operate together. Just as a business team is most effective when it contains individuals trained in all the essential functions of operating the business and when these people interact harmoniously with one another—so too, our lives are most successful when we have all the components necessary for a good life and when these components operate harmoniously with one another.

In our book, *The Holistic You,* we quote William James, often called the father of American psychology, who wrote in his 1890 work, *Principles of Psychology*:

> . . .*a man's Self is the sum total of all that he can call his, not only his body and his psychic powers, but his clothes and his house, his wife and children, his ancestors and friends, his reputation and works, his lands and horses, and yacht and bank-account. All these things give him the same emotions. If they wax and prosper, he feels triumphant; if they dwindle and die away, he feels cast down—not necessarily in the same degree for each thing, but in much the same way for all.*

James identifies the same basic 5Fs that we do, referring to Fitness and Faith in "his body and his psychic powers" and his Family, Friends, and Financial acquisitions in the words that follow. He understood that a human being is not simply a body, nor is he his money or his family. A whole human life is like a miniature world, with several key facets being crucial to his sense of completion.

Exercise 1.1

Pick one enterprise or item in your life upon which you rely. List 10 components (not in any particular order of importance) without which the entire system would be less efficient and possibly even cease to function. We will start you off with the example of a coffee shop.

Coffee Shop

1. Coffee growers

2. Crew to harvest the beans

3. Coffee bean processing equipment

4. Planes and trucks—transportation

5. Police force and societal norms that keep the shop a safe place to be

6. Cup, straws, napkin manufacturers

7. Staff

8. Refrigeration equipment

9. Banking system/investors

10. Internet system for taking orders and payment

Now, it is your turn:

1.
2.
3.
4.
5.
6.
7.
8.
9.
10.

Just as a business demands many parts that must work together, so does a complete life.

What Systems Have We Been Sold? Getting Rid of Our Myths of Happiness

Part of our goal in *The Holistic You* is to present a way of thinking that accustoms you to subject almost all conventional wisdom to critical analysis.

We've been taught, perhaps, that a highly individualistic, career-oriented life is the greatest thing to strive for. Alternatively, we might have been told that personal happiness and fulfillment is the most important goal. We encourage you to ask whether either of these are really the best recipe for your own success. Could there be some significant vacuum in the lives of people who aim for these visions?

Before we can reset our own thinking about what we wish to strive for, it is usually necessary to uproot the prevailing ideas around "the good life" that are swimming around in our minds. To this end, we'd like to invite you to engage in the following thought exercise.

Exercise 1.2

Identify what lifestyles or choices are being promoted by popular culture and media today.

These are the lifestyles you may be seeing in TV shows, online, within celebrity culture, or at a school or university campus. They are the unspoken assumptions about what's the "good sort of thing to do." Examples might include delaying having children, drinking heavily with friends, getting an advanced degree, traveling widely, finding your passion, or engaging in serial promiscuous sexual relationships.

1. _____

_____

2. _____

_____

3. _____

_____

4. _____

_____

5. _____

_____

Does your experience suggest that these lifestyle choices *deliver* what they *promise?*

Exercise 1.3

Some of us tend to be contrarian while others of us tend to be rule-followers. Some of us are "people-pleasers," while others of us delight in "pushing people's buttons." This is not necessarily easy to define. Going your own way might mean not following in the path of four generations of farmers or lawyers, but once you choose another direction, you may happily integrate and associate with those in your new profession.

Answering the following questions should illuminate how deliberate you are in your choices rather than responding with an inborn tendency.

1. Can you think of an instance when you were a teenager where your friends all wore the same brand, watched the same show, or played the same sport and you chose not to join in?

   _____

2. As an adult, have you ever taken a stand on an issue or voted in a way that was the opposite of your friends, family, or coworkers? Did you do so quietly, or did you articulate your position?

   _____

3. Are you able to politely listen with an open mind when someone is professing an opinion with which you heartily disagree? Can you think of an example when you did so?

   _____

4. Have you ever made a major break from your family or community? Did this sever relationships or were you all able to accept having different paths? In retrospect, do you think you did the correct thing? If it led to estrangement, could you have done anything to make it less contentious?

   _____

Reflections

Do you notice anything immediately after completing this exercise? Have you identified any values or lifestyles that you're not sure you are comfortable with but that you've unconsciously adopted because of the people around you?

If you feel a sense of doubt about whether these lifestyle choices are truly helping you, allow yourself to sit with that doubt. Do not run away from it. It may just be the opening through which a new, healthier, and vibrant way of living enters into your life.

Just as modern culture promotes certain ideas, it also promotes certain fears. The reaction of many governments and agenda-setters in society regarding COVID-19 certainly exacerbated fear in the hearts of many people. Warnings of dire outcomes from climate change greet us daily. On a personal level, many of us fear divorce and illness.

Can you identify fears that lurk in your heart? Has popular culture succeeded in injecting any fears into your being?

Exercise 1.4

List some of the fears that occasionally keep you awake.

1. _____

_____

_____

_____

2. _____

_____

_____

_____

3. _____

_____

_____

_____

The Secret of Ancient Jewish Wisdom

Ancient Jewish wisdom is a branch of knowledge based on the transmission of vital data handed down originally from God to Moses on Mount Sinai. This was then handed down teacher to disciple until the present time.

This is the guidance we bring to you in choosing how to live your life. We believe this wisdom comes from a tested source. There are many others who see any biblically based wisdom as backward and an impediment to success.

Before examining your views on various subjects, it is worth looking to see where those views originate. Take a deep look at your present values. Who have you been taking advice from? Who are the sources of influence in your life and the lives of the people who have an influence on you?

We all have things that we look to as reliable, whether we are conscious of them or not. Before we can reset any of our attitudes, it's important to become aware of where we are currently turning for our information—not just about what medicine to take for a given illness or what the best-performing vacuum cleaner this year might be (though those are important questions too!)—but about how to achieve a meaningful and happy life.

If I needed to learn how to operate a particular app on my phone, finding a video on YouTube might be sufficient. If I'm still confused, reaching out to a tech-savvy friend might be a reasonable next step. Finally, calling the customer service for the app and asking for clearer guidance might become necessary. The company, after all, is probably the highest authority on how to use its products.

When it comes to bigger questions, like knowing whether I should marry the person I'm currently dating, how to raise a healthy child, how many children to bring into the world, or who do I side with if my mother and my wife are arguing, and many more questions like this, where should I go? What about when it comes to structuring and thinking about my life as a whole? Is there a data source that can answer these questions?

We often don't think about *who* we are yielding authority to over parts of our lives. Particular people or institutions often exert authority over us without our even knowing it—ranging from our parents and communities, to the media and the culture we grow up in. Part of building a healthy, holistic life of our own means re-examining who sculpts our lives and what messages they are giving us.

Exercise 1.5

To start thinking about your beliefs and where they came from, take a moment to identify some of the key beliefs that you received from the following sources:

1. Your country of origin:

_____

_____

2. Your neighborhood or community:

_____

_____

3. Your parents' home/how you were raised:

_____

_____

_____

4. Your educators and teachers:

_____

_____

_____

5. Your friends and peers:

_____

_____

_____

Exercise 1.6

In reflecting on the beliefs that you received from these different sources, do you notice any resistance in yourself? Are these all ideas that you truly want to accept?

In the following table, list beliefs you want to keep, beliefs you want to let go of, and beliefs you're still not sure about.

Beliefs to Keep:	
Beliefs to Let Go Of:	
Beliefs I'm Not Sure About:	

How Holistic Systems Work

The same way that your car requires all its parts to work harmoniously together, so does your life. That's the secret behind *The Holistic You*. Your life is a *system* of integrated parts, which means that each part influences the others. Making one part of your life stronger may lift up all the other parts. Neglecting one part may bring the others down. Focusing too much in one area and not enough in others will throw things out of balance.

We suggested that the five pillars of a healthy life are the following (in no particular order):

1. **Family:** These are the relationships we have with parents, siblings, spouses, children, and other blood relatives or relatives through marriage. From another perspective, we speak of family as the relationships that result from sexual connection. When we share a joyful multigenerational family gathering, as awkward as it might be to think about, we sometimes forget that the only reason we are there with uncles and aunts and cousins is because many years ago, Grandpa and Grandma's eyes met, they formed a bond and later found ecstasy in one another's arms.

2. **Finance:** This covers relationships with our possessions and with our money in all its forms. It includes human connections that revolve around money. Employers, employees, customers and clients, work associates, professional associations, and vendors all fall under this pillar.

3. **Friendship:** This includes friends or people we connect with through shared interests like hobbies or sports, local events, or our children's education. Political and social groups with which we associate and charity organizations in which we actively participate also fall under this category. Likewise, the experience of "community" that many people feel through association to a religion is part of the friendship pillar. Most relationships with people who are linked to us neither through family nor money fall into this category.

4. **Faith:** Faith refers to our relationship with things that cannot be measured in a laboratory. Faith may be a commitment to integrity, say, or the love and esteem of others that we feel. Whatever beliefs play a role in our lives or set of values that governs our decision-making fall under the Faith heading as does, obviously, a relationship with God.

5. **Fitness:** This pillar refers to everything having to do with our bodies—our anatomy, physiology, and biology. Fitness covers our health and how we maintain it. How we eat, breathe, excrete, drink, make love, and eventually die are covered in detail in ancient Jewish wisdom.

Exercise 1.7

For each of your 5Fs, rate the following:

- The health of the 5F in your life, where 1 is *extremely unhealthy* and 10 is *extremely healthy*.

- How much of your energy and time do you currently invest into activities related to this pillar. Think about both how much time and how much active effort go into each pillar. Use the bar to fill out an amount, or write a percentage if that is more intuitive for you.

Candor and self-awareness are necessary preconditions for gaining most from this exercise.

Pillar	Health Rating 1–10	How Much Time and Energy Do I Invest?(minimal – excessive)
Faith		
Family		
Fitness		
Friendship		
Finance		

Reflections

Do you notice any mismatch after doing this exercise? Is possible that you consider your Faith category to be relatively healthy, but you in fact invest almost no energy into the spiritual aspect of your life?

Do you think you have a healthy Family life but give your spouse or children a relatively small amount of your time?

Pay attention to these mismatches. Sometimes we are mistaken about the true health of an area of our lives. It is possible that a particular area of your life may require more investment than you currently think.

Exercise 1.8

Take a moment to reflect on each of the 5Fs. What would a "healthy" version of this pillar look like in your life?

1. Faith:

_____

_____

2. Family:

_____

_____

3. Fitness:

_____

_____

4. Friendship:

_____

_____

5. Finance:

_____

_____

Building on the previous exercise, write down five things that you can do, starting this week, to strengthen one or more of the 5Fs in your life.

1. _____

_____

2. _____

_____

3. _____

_____

4. _____

_____

5. _____

_____

It is important for a thought to trigger an action. Sometimes, having too many projects overwhelms us, which brings about a passive torpor resulting in nothing actually happening.

Pick one of the five action points from the previous list that you believe that you will be able to implement starting now. Make sure it is very specific, actionable, and verifiable. Write it down! Place a tickler in your calendar for a week from today and check in to see how you did. Repeat with the same or a different action item.

Meeting the Five Fs

Crosslinks

Now let's think about another aspect of your life system, namely, its crosslinks. A crosslink is any interaction between two or more of the 5Fs in your life. For instance, for Finance–Friendship, you might notice that when you made some new friends, new work opportunities opened up, and you were in a position to possibly make more money.

Look at the following crosslinks, and jot down one or two ways that helping one 5F has benefited or might benefit the other.

Faith–Family:	
Faith–Finance:	
Faith–Friendship:	
Faith–Fitness:	
Family–Finance:	
Family–Friendship:	
Family–Fitness:	
Friendship–Finance:	
Friendship–Fitness:	
Fitness–Finance:	

It Helps to Play by the Rules of the Game

It is very hard to play a game without knowing the rules. Imagine arriving in a new country and needing to get a job. Do you know what is expected before and after the interview? Is it appropriate to email your interviewer directly? What kind of dress is expected? How should you compose your resume? Without checking in to find out these "rules," we are subject to making all sorts of gaffes, which may jeopardize our chance of winning the position.

Whatever we are engaged in, in life, it helps to play by the rules. So often, the rules are unspoken, and we understand them automatically. At other times, however, deep confusion about how to conduct ourselves can be a source of endless frustration and heartbreak.

The 5F system depends upon the idea that there are rules to how to live. Some ways of raising children are better than others. You can implement techniques to increase your income. Likewise, some ways of engaging with a spouse are better than others. Some life goals will likely lead to satisfaction. Others, to disillusionment.

That's why, if you want to be happy in your relationships and satisfied in your life, it's really helpful to know the rules of the game. But we don't always know the rules instinctively. Very often, we need to learn them from reliable mentors and sources. Learning wisdom in this way can truly transform our lives.

To help you feel just how true this is, take a few moments to complete the following exercise.

Exercise 1.9

Think of three times that the advice that someone gave you or a book you read changed your life.

1. _____

_____

_____

_____

2. _____

_____

_____

_____

3. _____

_____

_____

_____

Q Reflections

Now ask yourself—where would I be if I had never received this advice, or learned this wisdom? What mistakes would I still be making? Name three specific behaviors/habits you might still be doing if you hadn't learned not to from an outside source:

1. _____

_____

_____

2. _____

_____

_____

3. _____

_____

_____

This could be as simple as not knowing how to fold fitted sheets or failing to communicate properly when you are struggling with a heavy emotion.

Take a moment to appreciate the benefit to your life of no longer making these mistakes.

We look forward to continuing with you in the next chapter.

Chapter 2

Connect for Success

Think of life as a giant web. Strands of energy, created through mutual dependence and needs, snake between all life forms on our planet. Nothing that is living, by definition, could survive without a connection to something else. To live requires a being to *consume* something that feeds it life. And so, in our basic needs—whether for food, air, or water—we *must* be connected to something beyond ourselves to stay alive.

But basic needs for sustenance are just the tip of the iceberg. When we really think about what it takes to survive—to make it through tough winters, to create lasting shelter, to raise another generation—we see quickly that the more integrated we are in the web of connections with the physical world around us, and most notably, with other people, the more we have a fighting chance at making it. Connection is such a key to successful living that the prime characteristic shared by those on the fringes of society is nearly always lack of connection to others.

Isolation, on the flipside, is nearly always a mighty disadvantage. Though temporary periods of quiet introspection can be healthy for all of us (and perhaps you are engaged in this activity at this moment!), long-term isolation is extremely unhealthy. Animals that get separated from their herds are far more vulnerable to attack and hunger. Being disconnected from our friends and family, as many were during the COVID-19 pandemic, is detrimental to emotional and psychological well-being. When employees cease to communicate effectively with one another and either isolate or actively disconnect, company operations can become a shambles. Human isolation and disconnection remove us from life and render us vulnerable and unsatisfied.

This book is all about cultivating stronger connections. Three of our 5Fs revolve directly around connections that we have with other people. These are Family, Friendship, and Finance.

Exercise 2.1

List five things that only work because of their connections with other things. (These connections could be technical, mechanical, human, chemical—the sky is the limit. Examples might be a car, a construction crew, or a school.)

1. _____

2. _____

3. _____

4. _____

5. _____

Choose one of the items just listed. What happens when the connections holding this entity together start to falter?

_____

Connections in Time

Connecting in a healthy way means not only connecting to things that are present today but connecting to the past and to the future. To embed ourselves deeply in the web of life, such that we are firmly and securely held by our connections to the powers around us, we also need a connection to the people and ideas that came before us, which is where we were both physically and spiritually "conceived," and to the generations that lie ahead of us, those lives and the world that we are "conceiving" or bringing forth into being all the time.

The Holistic You: Workbook

Exercise 2.2

1. In what ways does having a connection to the past improve one's life?

_____

2. In what ways does having a connection to the future improve one's life?

_____

3. On a scale of 1–5, with 1 being *very weak*, and 5 being *very strong*:

    a. Rate your feeling of connection to the past: _____

    b. Rate your feeling of connection to the future: _____

4. What are three ways you might strengthen your connection to the past?

    a. _____

    b. _____

    c. _____

5. What are three ways you might strengthen your connection to the future?

    a. _____

    b. _____

    c. _____

6. Which of the listed actions are most practical for you to integrate into your life?

    a. _____

    b. _____

    c. _____

Reflections

Is connection to the past and future something you've ever thought about before? If it is, good for you! If not, what did you notice on this first attempt?

Sometimes, while completing this exercise, people discover that their connection to the past—whether it be through connection to family heritage or history as a whole—is surprisingly weak, even though we are only here as a result of what came before us!

Often, children acquire a sense of their connection to the past through their education. They learn about history from their teachers and about personal history from family. When we do not receive a strong education around the past, or when it is presented only in a negative light, we are at risk of feeling as though we're uprooted in our lives rather than firmly planted in a larger, more meaningful story that is unfolding. It is never too late to educate yourself if this is something you missed out on. Neither is it too late to make sure that those who follow you know their story. Nobody thrives as an orphan of time.

The Bible's Teaching of Connection

From the first verses of Genesis, the Bible stresses the importance of connection. In *The Holistic You* we provide important examples of this. The Bible is replete with tragedies that result from lack of proper appreciation of other people, starting with the tale of Cain and Abel and continuing through all the other books. Getting along with others is one of the most important talents we can cultivate and one of the hardest.

Before we explore our human connections, it's important to get a reading on how we feel toward other people in general.

Exercise 2.3

Rate the following statements from 1–5, where 1 is *rarely or never* and 5 is *all the time*.

1. Other people are annoying to deal with. _____

2. Most people I've known have disappointed me. _____

3. Other people make it harder for me to succeed. _____

4. I need to protect myself from the people around me. _____

5. Other people don't respect me._____

Add up your scores from each statement.

If you scored less than 10 on the previous exercise, you can skip the following exercise. If you scored 10 or more, it is worth answering the following questions:

1. Can you name up to three early experiences that made you inclined to distrust or dislike others?

a. _____

b. _____

c. _____

2. How could others in your life have behaved differently to maintain trust and integrity?

_____

_____

_____

3. In your own life, have you ever noticed a connection between how you treat others and how others treat you? Describe a time that you've observed this.

_____

_____

_____

4. Thought Exercise: Can you envision a set of relationships and interactions with other people that are predominantly positive and cooperative? What shared principles might need to be present to make this possible?

_____

_____

_____

_____

Reflections

As we go through this exercise, it is imperative to see that how positively we feel toward other human beings depends heavily on *how we conduct ourselves and they conduct themselves.*

When we are treated lovingly and fairly as children, we tend to grow up feeling worthy and secure. When we are treated harshly or abusively, we can internalize negative messages about ourselves while becoming suspicious of others.

Likewise, as adults, the way *we behave toward others* and the way *others behave toward us* will largely determine the quality of our relationships. Therefore, having firm principles about how to behave is crucial for developing strong relationships.

This exercise is meant merely as a starting place to unpack any negative feelings you may have toward other people. If this exercise resonated with you, you might want to seek out additional guidance, which may enable you to create more positive relationships with others. It is also worth contemplating whether your life would be enhanced by repairing older relationships that might have deteriorated and how you might accomplish this.

Family Connection

The first connections discussed in the Bible are family connections and these are usually the first and strongest connections that define our sense of Family. As families grow, they morph into tribes and nations that are too large for the people within them to know everyone individually. Our relationships with people outside our immediate or closely extended family are defined under Friendship and Finance.

Exercise 2.4

Take an inventory of the human connections in your life:

1. Count and give approximate numbers of the following:

- Close family members: _____

    (People you can comfortably reach out to if there's something you need)
- Friends: _____

    (The type of person who would pick you up from the airport in the middle of the night)
- Acquaintances: _____

    (People you interact with occasionally who are an extra source of connection in your life)

2. Looking back over your answers, think of the five strongest relationships in your life. List them here:

a. _____

b. _____

c. _____

d. _____

e. _____

3. What makes these relationships strong?

_____

_____

_____

4. How might you make them even stronger?

_____

_____

_____

_____

5. What can you do to bring the strengths of these relationships into other relationships in your life?

_____

_____

_____

_____

_____

Ⓠ Reflections

At the heart of any strong relationship is some kind of active investment of our energy. This is why you might have noticed the names of people you work with showing up on your list. If you work with someone over a long period, it's very possible that you actively engage with that person more than almost anyone else in your life.

Beyond this active engagement, consider the qualities behind the relationship. Which relationships wake up the most positive feelings for you? What are the qualities offered by the other person in that relationship? Respect? Listening and empathy? A willingness to prioritize your relationship?

As you see these positive qualities, think about how to imitate them within other relationships in your life.

Connection to Belongings

The 5F system encourages us to connect to other people. However, it also encourages us to connect with things. Many might think that owning things, wanting to own things, and enjoying owning things are all contradicted by the requirements of Faith. Some people mistakenly assume that faith leads to a life with no concern for owning "stuff." Interestingly, the Five Books of Moses are unequivocally in favor of private ownership. This is not to say that we should value things above people. However, not valuing things, or placing communal ownership over private ownership, is also a mistake.

Our possessions form an important extension of ourselves and forming healthy connections with these belongings is part of building a joyous and satisfying life. Caring for and maintaining our possessions is an important part of this area of connection and corresponds to the nurturing of relationships with people.

Exercise 2.5

List five possessions that add to your life:

1. _____

2. _____

3. _____

4. _____

5. _____

Take a moment to appreciate what they bring to your life.

Evaluate the relationship you have with more of the possessions in your life and list possessions that you would do well to dispense with.

_____

_____

How well are you maintaining your most important possessions?

List your three most valuable possessions and rate how well you care for each:

1. _____

2. _____

3. _____

The True Meaning of Harmony

Let's look at two ways that people have classically thought about peace and harmony.

In the first way, peace is thought to be a product of erasing boundaries. Imagine living in a house where no room belongs to any specific person, all clothing can be used by all the people living there, and likewise, everyone is equally responsible for all the tasks of the household—regardless of how suited they are for doing them. No one has any special affiliations to hobby groups, religious groups, or social groups. Everyone is part of the same group. There are no divisions among people. We have basically described a commune, taken to a bit of an extreme.

Does that sound good to you?

Here is a different way of thinking about peace. Everyone has clearly defined possessions and identities. In a household, the parents have a room, children have their own or shared rooms, and everyone has their own clothing. Some of the household members belong to sports teams, others to art or dance groups. Different people in the household fulfill different tasks, according to their station in the household and their natural ability. The individual members of the household, though each treated as a unique person, are expected to behave respectfully toward one another, to share, and to contribute to keeping the household running.

How does this one sound?

Though the first way of creating peace has enticed hippies, philosophers, and artists over the centuries, most of us know that it is a recipe for disaster. Ancient Jewish wisdom recommends the second path, based on boundaries.

True harmony is achieved when we respect the integrity and individuality of each person or each part of a system, and then learn to integrate those parts into one larger entity. Each of our organs must do its unique part in serving the body, yet all our organs are ultimately part of one, unified entity. In the same way, people achieve peace by fulfilling unique roles and functions within the world but still working to integrate themselves within a greater whole.

When it comes to achieving harmony in our lives, we need to integrate our 5Fs as well as keep them separate. Sometimes it can be tricky to ensure that we are not trying to achieve harmony by allowing different elements of life to bleed into one another in ways that violate the integrity of the parts, thus damaging the system.

Exercise 2.6

Read the following scenarios. On the left side are examples of ways in which a person might compromise the integrity of one of the five Fs by blurring the boundaries between that F and the others. On the right side are the same scenarios, but they have been corrected to protect the boundaries around each pillar.

Blurred Boundaries	Protected Boundaries
A father takes work calls while at dinner with his family. (blurring Family–Finance)	The father puts away his phone during family dinners to focus on his family.
A girl invites a close friend out to coffee and then surprises the friend by trying to sell her something. (blurring Friendship–Finance)	The girl openly shares her involvement with a new business with her friend rather than using a friendly coffee date to attempt a surprise sale.
During a prayer or meditation practice, a congregation member continually thinks about the party she plans to attend later rather than her connection with a higher power. (blurring Faith–Friendship)	The congregation member sets aside her thoughts about the party during her prayer/meditation practice.
A boss asks an employee on a date. (blurring Family–Finance)	The boss does not date employees. If he feels strongly about starting a relationship with an employee, he discusses it openly with her, and they consider terminating her employment before beginning a relationship.
A businessman enters into a business agreement with a friend casually, without taking the necessary precautions of writing a contract. (blurring Friendship–Finance)	The businessman draws up a contract when entering into any business agreement, even with friends and relatives.
A relative invites a close friend to a family vacation without confirming that her family is comfortable with the friend's presence. (blurring Friendship–Family)	The relative openly discusses her interest in inviting her friend with the rest of the family and defers to their wishes.

Blurred Boundaries	Protected Boundaries
A young couple borrows money from parents or family members without a strict intention of paying it back. (blurring Family–Finance)	The young couple take their family loans seriously and are diligent in repaying them.
Coworkers spend significant work time at the office chatting about non-work-related subjects. (blurring Friendship–Finance)	The coworkers arrange a time after work to socialize and keep interactions at the office focused around their work, unless it is during break times.

Now that you've gotten an idea what blurring boundaries between the 5Fs might look like, think of situations in your life where you may have been guilty of "blurring boundaries." Write them down. For your own eyes only.

1. _____

2. _____

3. _____

4. _____

5. _____

Reflections

The area of blurred boundaries when it comes to the 5Fs is admittedly tricky. The whole foundation of the 5F system is that all five pillars are intimately connected and intertwined. This can make it hard to determine when a crossover between two categories is healthy and encouraged, compared with when it is damaging.

In general, it is helpful to think of Family, Friendship, and Finance as separate tracks.

Though a person can, and often should, transition from one track to another within a given relationship, as in the case of investing in a family member's solid enterprise (Family > Finance) or forming a friendship with a coworker or employee (Finance > Friendship), the transition should generally be clear and marked.

Have you ever done a work project for a friend at a discounted price and then regretted it? Or gotten so close to someone you work with that you started to lower your professional standards in the way that you communicated with them? We are not recommending never to offer your friends discounts or build strong relationships with co-workers. We are simply advising that you be aware of what track you are operating within at any given time and adhere to the rules of that track. That means you cannot use your friends for financial gain, and you cannot be expansive in how you track your hours because you're working for a family member.

Chapter 3

Seeing the Invisible

D ifferent words mean different things to different people. In the United Kingdom, a "jumper" refers to a sweater. In the United States, a "jumper" is a sleeveless dress, typically worn over a blouse.

When we use the terms "faith" and "spirituality," it may trigger automatic associations for you. For many, faith is the act of blind belief in something that can't be known, and spirituality refers to an experience of either heightened consciousness or divine connection.

When we use these terms, we mean something slightly different.

Firstly, for the purposes of this book, the words faith and spirituality are used interchangeably. They refer to all aspects of our existence that cannot be measured or scientifically observed. Examples of spiritual concepts might include ethical principles, the experience of pleasure, music, love, loyalty, or a particular personality type or temperament. In other words, they relate to all things that are not clearly measurable by science.

This is not to say that science may not *try* to touch spiritual concepts, by creating operational definitions for them. For instance, to study depression, researchers will come up with a set of proxy measures that might include physiological or neurological markers and self-reporting, which can be measured and observed. Then, by monitoring these measures and following a particular treatment, they will pronounce the treatment either effective or ineffective at reducing depression.

In this way, science attempts to apply scientific principles to spiritual concepts. However, the truth is that depression remains an immeasurable experience in its essence. You cannot hold up a tape measure or microscope to it. It is experiential, and experiential things are subjective and usually spiritual.

Exercise 3.1

To gain some practice operating within our definition of spirituality, let's try a basic exercise. Here are five things we would consider "spiritual": happiness, motivation, love, integrity, and emotional needs.

List five more spiritual concepts:

1. _____

_____

_____

2. _____

_____

_____

3. _____

_____

_____

4. _____

_____

_____

5. _____

_____

_____

The Blindness of Science

Are blood pressure medication and vitamin E supplements the only treatment for a person with high blood pressure and low levels of the vitamin? Or could it be that this person is spending too much time indoors and too much time alone?

Are anti-depressants really the answer for the widow who is grieving the loss of her husband, or would a better prescription be a community of friends and family to help her pull through the stages of loss?

Because science can only measure the material aspects of life, it is often blind to the spiritual aspects of a situation, which may, in reality, be playing a significant role. This blindness appears not only in situations that deal strictly with science, but also in situations where the deeper aspects of a situation are ignored or neglected.

For instance, when a little girl is deeply distraught because she didn't collect as many prizes as her big brother, do we see the issue as only being about the prizes? Or do we see the deeper issue—that this little girl is always feeling overshadowed by her older brother?

When someone asks for a raise at work, do we see only the request for money? Or can we tell if there are deeper needs at play? Perhaps for greater recognition and responsibility?

When a customer walks into a store and asks for a particular item, does the saleswoman only hear the specific request? Or can she start to deduce the larger set of needs that the customer is interested in filling, which will make her far more incisive and successful in the suggestions that she makes to the customer?

Because science deals in materialism, it is so often blind to the deeper needs at play in a situation, the spiritual needs. In life, it is important to pay attention to the spiritual aspect of every situation and not to turn a blind eye toward these elements in life.

Exercise 3.2

In the following scenarios, write down what the possible spiritual needs might be.

1. A wife asks her husband to buy her a gift.

Possible spiritual need: _____

_____

_____

2. A man buys a large pickup truck to use in his construction business.

Possible spiritual need: _____

_____

_____

3. An employee who has been working overtime for several weeks, asks for an extended period of vacation.

Possible spiritual need: _____

_____

_____

4. A child asks his father to read him a book.

Possible spiritual need: _____

_____

_____

Reflections

Can you see the way that there might be many answers to the previous question? The child asking to be read to may be looking for attention from his father or he may be simply interested in alleviating his boredom. The man who purchases the pickup truck may wish to feel powerful and manly, or perhaps his primary concern is having a reliable vehicle for the work he needs to do.

When people only look at the surface of a situation, they are bound to miss so much of what really matters. It is only by inquiring more deeply and thinking about the spiritual side of every situation that we begin to appreciate the uniqueness of every situation and how to best address it.

Exercise 3.3

Even when dealing with largely physical phenomena, science does not always tell the truth, the whole truth, and nothing but the truth. Many ideas that scientists unequivocally touted in certain years later turned out to be wrong. We will start you off with one. List 3 more.

1. Exposure to radiation is good for your health.

2. _____

_____

_____

3. _____

_____

_____

4. _____

_____

_____

Human Origins

Everyone can appreciate the spiritual side of life according to our definition. When we write about Faith, connecting to and appreciating the spiritual aspect of all things is our intention.

Many consequences in our life and decisions we make flow from how we answer the question of how humans arrived here on earth—whether through a lengthy process of unaided materialistic evolution or as a consequence of a good and loving God creating us in His image and placing us on this planet.

The two alternative views about the origin of humanity also have implications about the future of humanity. One view envisages the eventual destruction of the planet and of humanity while the other view sees an ultimate redemption.

Wherever your instincts take you, the following exercises will assist you in knowing yourself, a vital pre-condition to life improvement. Take some time to get in touch with what you currently believe about human origins and what the implications of those beliefs are.

Exercise 3.4

Take a deep breath before you proceed, making sure to fully exhale. Plant your feet on the ground and relax. Then, complete each sentence as rapidly as possible.

If I am purely a physical being, then that means

_____

_____

If I have both physical and spiritual parts to me, then that means

_____

_____

People believe that science is the only source of truth because

_____

_____

People **don't** believe science is the only source of truth because

_____

_____

Deep down, when I ask myself what *I* believe about God, my answer is

_____

_____

Reflections

Doing this exercise correctly can be a powerful way to allow you to get in touch with your own inner set of values. How did it feel? Were you surprised by any of the answers or insights that you put down on paper?

If you struggled with this exercise and your mind felt blocked and unable to write, don't worry. Try to revisit it at another time when you are feeling more relaxed and less pressured.

A Thought Exercise

We are now going to move into a less intuitive and more thoughtful place.

Give yourself the time and headspace to really mull over the next question. Ask yourself: What are the implications of believing in a materialistic worldview, in other words, a worldview that only acknowledges the reality of physical things? Only things you can see and touch are part of reality.

After you've thought about that question, pause, and think carefully about its counterpart. Specifically: What are the implications of believing in a Divine Creator, who created the world and human beings within it? What are the implications of a world that is not purely materialistic but is also spiritual, and in which human beings are endowed with powerful divine souls?

When you've taken the time to think about these questions, write down the implications that you thought of.

Exercise 3.5

Implications of a Materialistic Worldview	Implications of a Godly Worldview

Reflections

Did you find your answers surprising?

Do you think that the average person is aware of the different implications of these worldviews?

Where a Godly Worldview Makes a Big Difference

Let us consider one specific area of life where belief in evolution versus creation has an incredibly strong impact—namely, family structure.

There is a very good reason for the rule of honoring parents being in the Ten Commandments. We can think of several reasons why parents ought not to demand respect or obedience. After all, should the autonomy of children be so violently wrenched away by domineering parents? Indeed, in some circles in which modern parenting is in vogue, parents are very reluctant to issue directives to their children.

By contrast, in a family shaped by a God-centric world view, parents teach their children that they, the parents themselves, are duty bound to obey their "Father in Heaven." In a similar way, children are duty bound to obey their earthly parents.

An evolutionary worldview does not encourage children to respect their parents. In many ways, evolutionary philosophy encourages me to consider myself superior, more advanced, than my parents. Whereas a creation philosophy has the reverse effect.

This analysis highlights one of the most powerful areas of life where the materialistic worldview has dramatic and often unexpected consequences—namely in the rearing of children.

The concept of respect and reverence for one's elders is present in every religious lifestyle. Yet in the secular worldview, it is much harder to justify. What is the outcome of this?

Exercise 3.6

Thought Exercise

1. What are the benefits of children respecting their parents?

_____

_____

_____

_____

2. In households where children are encouraged to see their parents as equal, or even less evolved than they are, what do children learn to believe about themselves and their place in the world?

_____

_____

_____

_____

Reflections

As you answer these questions, consider your own upbringing and the kind of authority your parents and teachers had in your life. Did they expect you to respect them? Were they people who were easy for you to respect? Or were your parents or teachers negligent, dishonest, or lazy in disciplining you? If so, how did that impact you? How would you have wanted them to behave differently?

Have you ever felt a desire for a strong mentor in your life, someone to guide and coach you through your life's challenges? Ideally, parents are the first mentors in a person's life.

Yet, how is mentorship possible if society adopts the attitude that younger generations are more evolved than the generations that came before them? The implications of believing that we do not need to learn from or look up to people who are older and wiser than ourselves are serious.

Can We Really Get Along Without God Awareness?

We emphasize that what you believe about God is entirely up to you. Nonetheless, faith in God, or the lack of it, strongly affects your interactions with the four other Fs. One important area of life impacted by faith or its absence is economics. The most powerful engine of human prosperity in the history of the world chose to place the words "In God we trust" not upon the walls of its churches but upon its currency. Among the many applications of faith to economics is the realization that every time a merchant extends credit to a customer, faith is being exercised.

Consider the role that faith plays in so many ordinary human interactions. Faith in God is a very specific and important subset of faith in general. Even acting on the assumption that tomorrow will be more like today than cataclysmically different from it is a manifestation of faith. When you provide a vendor with your credit card number, you employ faith that your purchase will reach your hands. When you hire a handyman to enter your home to effect repairs, you employ faith that he will do only good. When you bring a baby into the world, you employ considerable faith.

Exercise 3.7

Think of five areas in your day-to-day life where you employ faith:

1. _____

   _____

2. _____

   _____

3. _____

   _____

4. _____

   _____

5. _____

   _____

Will and Ariel Durant were acclaimed historians and philosophers. They wrote numerous best-selling books about the history of civilization.

Despite the Durants' personal rejection of religion, Ariel wrote that her husband harbored doubts about what "deposing God" might do to society. He wondered, "Could it be that all that enthusiastic slaughter of irrational creeds had undermined the secret foundations of civilization itself?"

In other words, could it be that by removing God from society, they and other philosophers had robbed civilization of the beliefs it needed to create lawful, moral, and even happy societies?

Faith, as it turns out, may be more important than modernity would have us think. For one, it seems to be a crucial belief for stepping into the future.

Imagine two people, one of whom runs a mile a day and works out with weights three times a week, while the other is a lazy person whose greatest physical exertion is to press the button on the television remote. On separate occasions, each of them witnesses a car accident. Both stop to help, and in each accident, a heavy part of a vehicle needs to be lifted off a trapped victim. Which individual will be more helpful? Clearly the runner who has built up his muscles at the gym will be better able to free the unfortunate driver. The other man, the couch potato, might stop and might even try to lift the axle assembly off the injured driver, but unless endowed with superhuman natural strength, he is unlikely to be able to achieve very much.

Now, imagine someone who "works out" her faith muscle by regularly connecting with God. Every time that person engages in prayer, it is an act of faith. Every time that person takes money out of her pocket and gives it to charity or a religious cause, it is an act of faith. Every time that person resists following her heart and instead, hearing God's voice, obeys it and follows her head; that is an act of faith.

Will this person have an advantage in life? Indeed, having developed his faith muscles so effectively, he has more ability to cope with the yet unseen than another person who, having developed no faith, can work only with what he can see and touch.

The future is always unseen. Deciding to commit to marriage is an act of faith. Someone with well-developed faith muscles will far more easily take that daunting but very necessary leap. Leaving a job in order to start a new business takes considerable faith. Even buying a home takes more faith than renting. All these happiness-inducing activities will always be easier and less stressful for the human being with well-developed faith muscles.

Exercise 3.8

1. Think about a time when you were afraid to do something. Perhaps it is something you are currently afraid of doing or something you did or didn't do in the past. Write it down: _____

2. How would you feel about this choice if you believed that this enterprise would meet with success?

   _____

   _____

   _____

3. How would you feel about this choice if you had a string of similar attempts that had worked well in the past or you understood why they did not work?

   _____

   _____

   _____

4. Is a lack of faith holding you back from moving into the future?

   _____

   _____

   _____

The Holistic You: Workbook

Reflections

If faith is a muscle, we can build it up over time. Part of how we build this muscle is by habitually stepping into the unknown.

Entrepreneurs who develop new opportunities for value-creation in the world typically have to develop strong faith muscles. So do parents, who put themselves on the line for the next generation, without knowing anything about the child they will have before he or she is born. Visionaries and leaders have to have strong faith muscles to see a future that has yet to unfold and to believe they can make it possible.

We are not suggesting being foolhardy or reckless when making a decision. We should always do what we can to research a situation before making a leap of faith. But there is usually a faith component, even to the most well-researched and carefully thought-out decision, which can terrify and stymie people who have weak faith muscles. We can all become more comfortable with future unknowns if we become accustomed to embracing the idea of Faith.

Exercise 3.9

From 1–10, with 1 being *I am very afraid* and 10 being *I am not at all afraid,* rate how comfortable you are with taking a risk and stepping into the unknown.

I am very afraid   *I am not at all afraid*

   1   2   3   4   5   6   7   8   9   10

Where might you take small steps into the unknown in your life, in order to give yourself consistent, small wins?

- Maybe striking up a conversation with a stranger?
- Maybe giving charity, even if you feel afraid to give away money?
- Maybe looking at the decisions that you're not making, and taking one small action that will bring you closer to them?

Write down three possible steps to strengthen your faith muscle.

1. _____

2. _____

3. _____

Pick one of the three and set a goal to work on this area. Calendar a weekly check-in with yourself to see how you are doing.

Prescriptive vs. Descriptive

As we explain in *The Holistic You*, laws can be divided into two categories, prescriptive and descriptive. Prescriptive laws can be made and changed. They reflect cultures and community preferences. Descriptive laws are not decided arbitrarily by bureaucrats; they describe immutable realities.

Exercise 3.10

Which of these laws are descriptive and which are prescriptive? Write D or P on the line after the statement.

1. No loud noise after 10 p.m. _____

2. Do not exceed a 35-mph speed limit ___

3. Magnetism ___

4. The second law of thermodynamics ___

5. Separate glass bottles from other trash ___

We suggest in our book, that if God created man and the Bible is the instruction manual for humanity, then many of God's rules that seem arbitrary and prescriptive are actually descriptive of how human beings will best function.

Exercise 3.11

How might following this Biblical law lead to happier living?

1. Get married: _____

_____

_____

2. Be fruitful and multiply: _____

_____

_____

3. Distance yourself from falsehood: _____

_____

_____

4. Use honest weights and measures:_____

_____

_____

Chapter 4

Bodybuilding

Numerous studies have shown that social isolation is associated with increases in all-cause mortality risk to the same degree as smoking or high cholesterol levels. Individuals tend to die after rather than before their birthdays and major holidays, suggesting some ability to postpone death for a short period to reach a meaningful goal. Conversely, depression and the associated social withdrawal/alienation is an independent predictor of shorter survival with cancer and heart disease.... We are social creatures, and we manage stressors better when we are not alone with them.

Professor David Spiegel, Chair of Psychiatry and Behavioral Sciences at Stanford

This type of observation is one of the many observations we make about Fitness. In our book *The Holistic You*, we explore the ways that our physical well-being is (not surprisingly) tied into the other components in our 5F system, namely Finance, Friendship, Faith, and Family.

How Fitness Is Impacted by the Other Four Fs

Many studies show a link between marriage, good health, and mental well-being. Single people also benefit from a strong network of relationships.

On the flipside, being physically fit makes us better able to engage with our families and friends—whether by tossing our kids up into the air or volunteering for our local church or synagogue by delivering heavy boxes of food donations.

And we need scarcely be reminded that healthy finances often correlate with better physical health. At the very least, a robust bank account provides a person with a sense of security that majorly reduces unhealthy stress in life. Financial health means the ability to take care of physical needs as they arise, whether to see a specialist or to repair a broken roof.

As we have seen, all of the 5Fs are interconnected, and Fitness is no exception. To fully appreciate the importance of our physical health and the ways that it is affected by and affects our other 5Fs , let's look at the way we experience our fitness a little more closely.

Exercise 4.1

1. Think of a time in your life that you felt the most physically fit. What was going on in your life? How about in your other four Fs?

_____

_____

_____

_____

_____

2. Think of a time in your life that you struggled with your physical health. What was going on in your life? How about in your other four Fs?

_____

_____

_____

_____

_____

Now we're going to approach this question in another way.

Exercise 4.2

If you struggle with fitness and health, especially on an ongoing basis, can you identify which of your other four Fs might be hurting? You may select more than one.

1. **Faith:** Example: I may have unresolved emotional trauma, confusion, or difficulty accepting myself. I may have existential anxiety because I do not feel I can trust in a Higher Power.

2. **Family:** Example: I may have tense family relationships, or I haven't been able to build a lasting relationship with a committed partner.

3. **Friendship:** Example: I am lonely often and do not have strong, close bonds with non-family members.

4. **Finance:** Example: I struggle financially and never feel able to cover my costs.

5. **Fitness:** All of my other four Fs are healthy. My fitness issues are truly related to diet, sleep, exercise, or illness.

Reflections

As you think about your fitness in relation to your other four Fs, what do you notice? Do you tend to isolate any health challenges that you've experienced solely to the Fitness pillar? Or can you see how these health challenges might be connected to broader needs in your holistic system?

If you selected number 5 in the exercise, be careful. There are many times where apparently genetic or incurable issues are cured with a holistic treatment and approach. At the same, there is no doubt that if you are facing major health challenges, your physical health may be at the root of the challenges you're experiencing in the other pillars. Committing yourself to searching for a treatment modality that will work for you is worth the effort.

Building Stronger Relationships

We hear a great deal today about an epidemic of loneliness. With people spending more time unmarried, opting not to have children, and leaving religious institutions that historically provided a base for friendship and community, many people today are lonelier than ever. Not surprisingly, this has a deleterious effect on their health.

In *The Holistic You,* we explained that being a friend is based in obligation. A friend is a person who sees himself as obligated to another—to show up for that person in times of need. The way we acquire strong friendships in our own lives, not surprisingly, is by learning to be good friends to other people.

If you struggle with loneliness on an intermediate or frequent basis, it is worth making an active effort to build stronger relationships with others—whether they be family members, coworkers, or friends.

Exercise 4.3

1. One a scale of 1–5, with 1 being rarely and 5 being very often, how frequently do you feel lonely?

1   2   3   4   5

2. Are there people with whom you wish you had a closer relationship? Write down their names.

   a. _____

   b. _____

   c. _____

3. What small action could you take to build stronger relationships with any of these people?

_____

_____

_____

4. Examine some of your relationships. How would those people describe your degree of dedication to the relationship?

   Do you think that you give more than you receive in your relationships, or do you think you are more of a beneficiary? Explain.

_____

_____

_____

Reflections

No matter how good your relationships currently are, they can always be better. Take this opportunity to identify new ways to strengthen your commitment to being a better friend.

　　Commit your thoughts to paper here:

Healing the Soul to Heal the Body

A friend of ours told us this story. She suffered from painful eczema on her hands. It was so pervasive, that she found herself bandaging all her fingers to avoid having the painful blisters pop as she typed on her computer.

One day, she met a hypnotherapist who was versed in past-life regression. The therapist hypnotized her, and she described how she visited a scene, supposedly from a past life, in which her hands were horribly injured. While under the hypnosis, her eczema burned brightly red. Following the hypnosis, it subsided significantly and proceeded to almost completely disappear from her hands. Though she occasionally experiences a flare-up, her issue was almost entirely resolved.

Though we are not trying to make a statement for or against the concept of past-lives and past-life regressions, we think this is a powerful demonstration of the way that the soul impacts the body. The hypnosis was directed at her *mind*. It did nothing whatsoever to her hands. And yet her hands were healed through an experience in her brain. We are familiar with other similar accounts.

There are good reasons to believe that mental and spiritual factors influence our health. Whether those factors are stress or depression, or how much we believe something will help (as with the placebo effect), how we think and feel will manifest in our body in some way.

In *The Holistic You*, we discussed the soldier who could only move his arm after processing his PTSD from not having given his dying friend some water. We looked at the surprising incidence of healing warts through hypnosis, and the way that athletes succeed through their mental determination, not just their physical prowess. And we noted that placebos have a surprising ability to heal us.

We can take away some principles from these stories:

1. Emotional trauma can physically diminish our physical health.
2. Our subconscious beliefs can hurt or heal our body.
3. Every physical challenge is also a mental challenge.
4. If we believe something has the power to help us, it often can.

Exercise 4.4

Thought Exercise

List other situations in which one or more of these principles apply—either from your own life or from something you have read or heard about.

1. _____

_____

_____

2. _____

_____

_____

3. _____

_____

_____

4. _____

_____

_____

5. _____

_____

_____

Reflections

As you look at these scenarios in which the mind has a clear impact on the body, do you notice other principles that you would add to our list?

Perhaps you noticed the way that your mind impacts your body in your own life. You might get an upset stomach when anxious. Or you might develop a skin rash in response to stress, or feel depressed if you go too many days eating highly processed foods.

Feel free to ponder this and jot down ways to deal with these physical symptoms through working on your emotions and thoughts in the following space.

_____

_____

_____

_____

_____

_____

_____

_____

Healing the Body to Heal the Soul

Not surprisingly, just as we see that healing the soul can heal the body, we see that the relationship works in the other direction as well. Not only do our minds affect our bodies, but our bodies also affect our minds.

Simple actions like smiling, exercising, and laughing palpably impact our mood and mental state.

Next time you feel down, consider doing one of the following to harness the power of body to heal the soul:

1. Listen to upbeat music and dance.
2. Enjoy some fresh air and physical activity.
3. Eat healthy, fresh foods.
4. Hug someone.
5. Smile. Laugh.
6. Achieve a victory—set yourself a small task, like doing 10 push-ups, and do it! You may discover you're ready to conquer another challenge with a small win under your belt.

Exercise 4.5

1. Do you have a go-to physical activity that improves your mental state? What is it?

_____

_____

_____

2. How often do you do this activity? _____

_____

_____

3. Can you incorporate 5–10% more of this activity into your life?

_____

_____

_____

The Golden Mean

Exercise is a crucial way that we take care of both our bodies and our souls. Historically, exercise was built into every person's daily routine—from tending to crops or animals to doing the laundry. Today, we need to actively make sure our bodies are engaged and are not trapped behind desks and steering wheels for the bulk of the day.

This does not mean that we are encouraging everyone to become a body-builder or so diet-conscious that they can never enjoy a meal with friends. We need to have a balanced relationship with fitness, one in which we focus on protecting and caring for our bodies, without placing our physicality above everything else.

Personal grooming is also important. How others perceive us greatly impacts how they respond to us. Being well dressed and well groomed are virtues. However, buying only designer items when you can't afford them or refusing to go out if you don't own the latest style would be going to an unhealthy extreme.

How can we find a balanced way to care for our bodies?

1. Identify your own pattern:

My current level of exercise tends to be:

Too little   Just right   Possibly overboard

The current degree to which I focus on my appearance tends to be:

Too little   Just right   Possibly overboard

2. If you answered either "too little" or "possibly overboard," take a moment to think about the costs. What are you missing out on by doing these activities either too little or too much?

_____

3. What small action could you take to either increase or decrease (as you need) your exercise and grooming, to come to a more balanced place?

Exercise: _____

Grooming: _____

_____

A note on exercise. If you are the type of person who finds it hard to incorporate exercise into your life, think about activities that are both easy and enjoyable to add to your day.

- Do you enjoy working in your garden? Make a point of spending some time doing that every day or a few days a week.
- Do you enjoy walking with a friend, or walking while listening to a favorite book or music? Do that more often.

We all do more of the activities that we enjoy and tend to avoid the things that we dislike.

You may find that the more you do of an activity, the more you will like doing it.

Food: Filling and Fulfilling

If you've perused the aisle at a grocery store recently, you have probably seen magazine covers featuring some new secret to weight loss and healthy eating. Messages about how to lose weight and get control of our food habits abound. Why is this such a popular subject?

The way that God introduces Adam to the Garden of Eden involves a dual injunction around food. "Of every tree of the garden you must eat, you must eat" (Genesis 2:16). We explained that the reason for this dual injunction is that eating is, in fact, a dual act. It works best when it is both physical and spiritual.

As we know from our earliest relationship with eating as breastfeeding babies, the time we spend drinking milk provides us with more than calories. As the baby nestles up to her mother, she is engulfed in a feeling of warmth and closeness. Eating is how we bond with our caretaker and how we get not only physical, but spiritual and emotional nourishment.

When we struggle with our eating habits, often it is because, though we may be taking in the physical calories and nutrients, we are failing to derive the spiritual benefit from food. To this end, we offered advice in our book on how to make eating a more spiritual act in your life.

 **Exercise 4.7**

Referring to Chapter 4 in the book, look at the tips we give for spiritual eating. Do one or two of them jump out at you as areas where you can improve?

1. What has prevented you from practicing these positive habits until now?

_____

_____

2. Can you deal with these barriers, perhaps by making a small change? What change would this be?

_____

_____

Breaking Bread with Brothers

One of the tips we discuss in *The Holistic You* is trying to eat with other people as often as possible. Yet, in our day, eating with others seems difficult. Perhaps you work at home and don't regularly see other people during the day. Perhaps it seems like there is never enough time to sit down and enjoy a leisurely meal with conversation.

Though we acknowledge these challenges, it is still worthy to strive for the ideal and to aim to eat with others on a semi-regular basis. Even if you are not having lunch with someone every day, can you perhaps share a dinner? If that still seems too ambitious, can you eat with other people two or three times a week? If you rarely eat with others, maybe aiming to eat with company once a week is the right place to start.

Once you commit to eating with others, you may be surprised by how much you enjoy it and want to increase the opportunities.

Exercise 4.8

List five people you could reach out to and share a meal with.

1. _____

2. _____

3. _____

4. _____

5. _____

List three questions (that don't involve gossip or complaining) that you might enjoy discussing with someone as part of your table conversation.

1. _____

2. _____

3. _____

Choose one name and one question to begin with. Open your calendar and decide on a time to invite this person to join you for a meal. Send the invitation.

Reflections

Imagine for a moment that you ate with other people at least once a day and always had meaningful table discussions—whether about ideas or art or travel or family life or politics or literature. What would the impact of this be on your eating habits? What would the impact of this be on your life?

Let this sink in. We hope you are feeling motivated to find more ways to include eating with others into your regular routine.

Speech: Unique to Humans

Not everybody has the gift of gab, but everyone can improve their ability to converse, talk, articulate, and persuade. Speech sets things in motion. Whether it is an idea for a financially productive collaboration, the launching of a friendship, or planting the seeds of a romance, nothing happens until someone creates words and someone else accepts those words into his or her being.

Often without realizing it, people judge each other by their speech. Having a varied vocabulary, speaking smoothly, not speaking in a monotone—all these will increase the likelihood that you will make connections that will improve your life.

Be wary of obscenities. It is almost impossible to avoid hearing or reading vulgar speech today unless you proactively banish it from your life. Using obscenities is a lazy way of expressing yourself. They get dropped into speech as nouns, as adjectives, and thrown into sentences at random. If you accustom yourself to using curse words, it is possible that when you need to speak without them, perhaps in an interview or while trying to sell a product, you may control your mouth, but your mind will be racing to find the right replacement word leading to a momentary pause in communication. Your listener will subconsciously notice the pause and perceive you as insincere.

Even if you monitor what you watch, watching a screen, be it a handheld device or a big screen TV, is an entirely different activity from reading or listening without engaging the eyes.

Do the following exercise over the course of a week, then repeat, repeat, repeat.

Exercise 4.9

1. How many hours this week did you spend being entertained by moving images on a screen? _____

   Don't guess the answer. Use a timer and be excruciatingly honest with yourself. (This may be one of the most painful exercises in this book.) The answer is nearly always higher than you would have guessed.

2. How many hours this week did you spend reading? _____

3. How many hours did you spend listening to a speech, class, or podcast?

4. Did any of these activities feature curses or vulgar language?

   Once you have a baseline, move on to positive actions. Work on reducing both your screen time and your exposure to vulgar language. At the same time, the following activities will increase your vocabulary and verbal fluency.

Exercise 4.10

1. Read aloud for 30 minutes three times a week. You can read to yourself or to others—this is one of the benefits of being around children. Children's books allow you to use different voices and focus on sounding interesting without struggling with vocabulary.

2. Once you are comfortable with reading aloud, use at least one of the weekly sessions to slowly increase the quality of your reading material.

3. Listen to speeches of famous orators from history, such as those of Winston Churchill. Ask yourself what made these speeches effective enough to influence the course of history.

4. Switch the proportion of time spent watching screens and time spent reading or listening.

Bodybuilding

The Other End of the Mouth—The Indignity of "Crap"

The mouth and the rectum are opposite ends of the same GI tract. In this way, they represent opposite ends of a continuous spectrum. On one end we find the mouth, the organ dedicated to speech. While the mouth ingests food, a physical commodity, it puts out speech, which is a spiritual commodity. Animals communicate, people speak. On the other end is the rectum, where purely material waste leaves the body. It ejects matter from which all goodness has been extracted.

When people identify themselves with "crap"—either through their language or behavior, they are rendering an assault on human dignity. It may seem like a small thing, but such an assault is insidious over time.

This assault can be added to the slew of behaviors that push us toward the animalistic side of ourselves, which causes a lamentable catalog of problems. Pay attention to prevent veering toward our more base urges.

We are surrounded by vulgar and profane language today in almost every public setting. Each time we hear a word, we react less strongly to it. Eventually, we can find ourselves using that language. Much of vulgar language revolves around bathroom activity.

Exercise 4.11

1. Raise your level of awareness. While in the supermarket, office, or on the street become conscious of the language surrounding you.

2. Catch yourself as you speak. Is your language refined or has profanity become part of your norm?

3. What action can you take to move closer to the "mouth" or spiritually dignified side of this spectrum?

4. Do you feel strong enough to let your friends and family know that you are guarding your language and your ears and you would appreciate their help while around you?

Reflections

Most of us can use work in this area. Even if we have a lot of work to do, we should not despair. Small, but consistent resolutions make a big difference over time.

The Spiritual Message of Sleep

Have you ever the expression "I'll sleep on it" as a way of dealing with a problem? Seems strange to think that disconnecting from our consciousness for several hours during the night would have a positive impact on an issue that presumably requires focus and intention to resolve.

Yet we know that sleep can help us solve problems. The same is true for symbolic sleep or breaks in our day or week. Stepping away from a project for a few hours can rejuvenate the mind so it is in better shape to approach the project again upon returning. Likewise, celebrating a weekly Sabbath does not deprive us of one-seventh of our creativity but bolsters our creativity for the other six days of the week.

Human creativity thrives in an environment of activeness, rest, and then activeness again. Apply effort, relax, and again apply effort. That is the pattern of creativity. Thrust and withdraw, thrust and withdraw. This process defines all acts of creativity.

Exercise 4.12

1. Do I incorporate enough downtime into my life, or perhaps too much? Circle one of the following. I need:

More downtime   No change. I have   To be more active
                 balanced activity and rest

2. If you have an imbalance in this area of your life, how might you begin to correct it by taking more downtime? Downtime could be an activity such as sleeping or meditating, but it could also be taking a walk in nature or playing with a child. The point is to stop actively focusing on whatever is consuming your mind.

3. Before you go to bed tonight, clear your mind of any problems you are facing. Some people find that writing them down is helpful, while the same activity makes others focus on them. Get to know your own pattern. Keep pen and paper reachable during the night in case you wake up with a fresh thought.

Resistance and Struggle

A great deal of modern society tries to make life as easy as possible. There are classrooms where parents call to complain if their child gets less than a grade of A, regardless of how much the student knows. Even in the US military, expectations are continually downgraded. It is as if we believe that life should be easy and without friction.

Instead, both our bodies and our souls thrive with struggle. Astronauts who are in a gravity-free environment suffer physically. A limb encased in a cast for too long becomes weak. If we never exert effort to show gratitude, tell the truth, or keep our temper, we are less capable to doing so when necessary.

Exercise 4.13

1. Have you ever avoided a major life-step such as marriage or a promotion at work because you were concerned that the effort to be successful would be too hard?

2. What is one area of your life where you feel you should be exerting yourself more?

_____

_____

_____

_____

3. Often, focusing on the pleasure we will derive from our exertion makes it easier to start than if we only focus on the pain. What pleasure will you derive from the effort you would employ?

_____

_____

_____

_____

Reflections

Life, as we know, is all about balance. Just as we need downtime, we need exertion. And it is worthwhile to welcome the pain of effort into life and not to run away from it.

The best way to do this is to realize that the flipside of pain is pleasure. Everything that matters most in life will be a little painful to accomplish.

Chapter 5

Money and Morality

S ome things can be stockpiled: canned goods, ammunition, bottled water. And if you store these items safely, you will have the same amount of whatever you stored months later as you had when you put them away. And those cans will be able to feed the same number of people, the ammunition will be good for the same number of shots, and so on.

But money does not work this way. If you stockpile your money, stashing thousands of dollars away in suitcases in your basement, will you have the same amount of money when you dig it up months or years later? You may have the same *number* of dollars. But will that money have the same purchasing power? Will you be able to exchange it for the same number of items at the store? The chances are that you won't.

The reason for this is that money, at its essence, is not a physical thing. Rather, it is a physical representation of something spiritual—namely, value. And as the value of money goes up and down with inflation, those dollars piled in your basement, however static and unchanging they appear to be, are actually fluctuating in their worth all the time.

Understanding the spiritual nature of money is the first step to really tapping into its power. To get in touch with this, we need to be in the habit of focusing on the *value* that money represents, and the value that creates money, rather than focusing on the physical manifestation of that value—namely, dollars and cents.

Exercise 5.1

List five different purchases you have made. These could be items you bought or fees you paid people to assist you with a service. Choose a range from inexpensive to expensive.

Thinking about this item or service, what would you have been willing to pay for it? Why is the value equal to or more than you paid, or alternatively, why do you feel you overpaid? We'll start you off with an example.

1. What you bought, and what you paid: _installation of washer/dryer; $150 ___

What would you have been willing to pay: _$200.00 _____

Why? Having someone competent and courteous do the installation rather than having to figure it out myself is worth more to me than I paid.

2. What you bought, and what you paid: _____

What would you have been willing to pay: _____

Why? _____

3. What you bought, and what you paid: _____

What would you have been willing to pay: _____

Why? _____

4. What you bought, and what you paid: _____

What would you have been willing to pay: _____

Why? _____

5. What you bought, and what you paid: _____

What would you have been willing to pay: _____

Why? _____

Reflections

Is the *value* you receive in a purchase something that you think about often? Do you notice that some purchases provide you with greater value than others? Why?

If you were in the habit of always thinking about the *value* behind a purchase, do you think you might change your spending habits? In what way?

Exercise 5.2

Consider three times you have been paid for work. Put down a specific job that you did rather than a general category of work.

What were you paid? What do you estimate was the value that you delivered to your customer or employer?

1. _____

2. _____

3. _____

Can you see ways that you could bring more value, and receive more money, for the work that you do?

_____

Let's Connect

If value is created when people serve one another in meaningful ways, then it goes without saying that the easier it is to connect with others, the more wealth creation is possible.

This is why every new technological development that makes it easier for people to connect with one another has created meteoric rises in prosperity. But while a greater quantity of connections can translate directly into more wealth, in the form of more sales to more customers, or in today's world, more likes by more subscribers, the quality of our connections still matters.

We shared the story of our friend Meir, a provider of disposable tableware for parties and entertainment. During the supply chain disruptions of 2020 and 2021, many of his competitors bemoaned the fact that they were not receiving their usual product from overseas. But Meir was somehow immune to this disruption. He had worked to cultivate strong personal relationships with all his suppliers, and when they had to choose to whom to send their limited quantities of product, they chose him.

Exercise 5.3

Take a moment to assess the quality of your finance-related connections.

Positive

1. Think of a time when someone you work with made the effort to build a strong and positive connection with you. What behaviors did that person do to build your level of connection? (If you don't have a real-life example, imagine what someone might do to build a strong relationship with you.)

_____

_____

_____

2. Think about the work relationships that you currently have that you might like to strengthen. This can include people you work for, with, or people who work for you. What steps can you take to strengthen these relationships?

_____

Negative

1. Think of a time when you were determined *not* to work with someone a second time. What behaviors caused this person to lose your trust?

_____

_____

_____

2. Think about the work relationships that you currently have. This can include people you work for, with, or people who work for you. Have you sometimes been guilty of negative behaviors that might cause them not to want to work with you?

_____

Reflections

As you do these exercises, pay attention to general trends. We all have strengths and weaknesses when it comes to working with other people. Some people are extremely timely and reliable but may be more uptight. Others may have an easy time building trust but may be a little more scattered in their work.

Do you notice any trends in your relationships? Are there things you are great at doing and other areas in which you generally struggle?

If there are, first take a moment to acknowledge the strengths you have already. Think about all the blessings they have brought you in your work and in your life.

Now turn to your weaknesses. Is there something you can do to strengthen yourself in these areas?

Exercise 5.4

Is there a store you dread going to? A company whose helpline you never want to call? Conversely, are there stores where you enjoy shopping? Have you ever gotten off a phone call with a company and felt delighted with how they treated your question or problem?

For one week, jot down various interactions you have with businesses or service providers, ranging from getting a morning coffee to dealing with your accountant. What made these interactions pleasant or unpleasant? Aside from the technical matters (getting coffee, filing taxes), some of which are inherently more pleasant than others, what put a smile on your face or left you dissatisfied?

1. _____

_____

2. _____

_____

3. _____

_____

4. _____

_____

5. _____

_____

 **Exercise 5.5**

Review what made certain stores, businesses, and individuals a pleasure to deal with and what made you want to avoid other stores, businesses, and individuals. How can you change the way you act to make it more likely that others will want to do business with you?

Collaboration

Our connections with other people can create outsized financial rewards in another way. What's the difference between one guy tinkering with an idea for a tech startup in his garage and a multimillion-dollar corporation like Apple? On some level, the answer is simple: the degree of connections involved in the enterprise.

Have you ever noticed that when a business moves from being a lone venture to involving a partnership with one or more people, it becomes greater than the sum of its parts? It's not just about having more skill sets on board; it's about the holistic system that develops when multiple people pool their talents to work toward a single goal. There is a synergistic effect of this. And when we multiply this synergistic effect across larger groups of people, the power of a business can grow exponentially.

Don't get us wrong here. We all recognize that sometimes companies can be mired in inefficient practices and perform poorly. We would say, in those cases, something in the holistic system is off. Maybe it's one crucial component—like staff motivation. Maybe it's several—like an unclear company vision, unethical practices, no accountability, and poor communication. Or maybe it's simply that the components of the business aren't well integrated with one another.

Bill Gates aptly stated, "The first rule of any technology used in a business is that automation applied to an efficient operation will magnify the efficiency. The second is that automation applied to an inefficient operation will magnify the inefficiency." In other words, more complex systems also have the potential to be more poorly run. Whenever we magnify a system, we also magnify its inefficiencies. We must therefore be careful to set up our systems well.

However, fear of a more complex system should not cause us to shy away from partnerships, whether in the form of a simple collaboration, a mentorship, a business partnership, or otherwise, which can greatly expand our potential.

Exercise 5.6

Whether you've noticed it or not, potential financial partnerships unquestionably exist in your life currently—perhaps with a coworker, a competitor, or a friend.

Let yourself think about your connections broadly. Then write down the names of five people with whom you could collaborate to generate financial benefit for you both.

1. _____

2. _____

3. _____

4. _____

5. _____

Choose one (or more) of the names on your list. What kind of value could the two of you create together that you could not create as individuals?

_____

What would need to happen for this collaboration to become a reality? What steps should you take to make it happen?

_____

Reflections

As you reflect on this activity, do you notice yourself feeling surprised by what you wrote down? Or is a financial collaboration something that has already been on your radar for some time?

Language Matters

Throughout *The Holistic You*, we emphasize how the language we use affects our thoughts. In the book, we recounted our friend Oscar's story where his competitors banded together to help him recover after a disastrous fire at his plant. This type of caring is not how business owners tend to be depicted in popular culture. In fact, successful people are often spoken about as if money is proof of greed and immorality.

Exercise 5.7

Sharpen your ears to catch how wealthy businesspeople are spoken about in movies, written about in books, and described by politicians. Write down biased language that you come across.

Once again, we will start you off.

1. (wealthy people) must "pay their fair share"

2.

3.

4.

5.

Reflections

It is much harder to do well at something that makes us feel ashamed. If we believe that charging for our products or services is akin to taking money from someone rather than conducting a fair and honest transaction, we will hesitate to name a price.

Be on the alert for attempts to make you feel immoral for being in business. When you hear language that demeans business or profit, counter it with telling yourself (aloud if possible) why it is prejudiced and wrong language.

Earning Money Versus Receiving Money

We understand the idea behind the aphorism, "Money can't buy happiness." Like all short and pithy statements, it holds both a kernel of truth and also some misleading thinking. If the money you earned represents having added to someone else's life, then it can contribute greatly to your happiness. There is a difference between just getting money and earning it.

Exercise 5.8

If you are raising children, this exercise may realistically depict decisions you are making today. If not, consider it a thought experiment.

Assuming that you wish to raise your children with a realistic understanding of money and its value, do you agree or disagree with the following statements? Why?

1. It is wrong for parents to use money as a means of influencing children's behavior.

2. Allowance should be based on age alone.

3. Children should be paid for any chores they perform.

4. Children should have a choice as to whether they give to charity from their allowance or not as well as how much they give.

5. A child's only jobs are to go to school and play.

6. Children should write a thank-you note before being allowed to use any gifts they receive from relatives or friends.

Reflections

We are not going to share our answers to these questions. Most of them do not have a simple yes or no answer. They are meant to spark conversation with your spouse, future spouse, and yourself.

Chapter 6

Sex: Pleasure and Pain

Until now, we've managed to keep three of our five Fs relatively contained within their own chapters. We discussed spirituality and Faith, we touched on Fitness, and we probed Finance, aiming to deepen our understanding of each of these pillars and begin to see some of the ways that they affect and interact with the other 5Fs. Although sex is not one of our 5Fs, it is an elephant in the room that does affect, aid, and disrupt our lives.

1. In your own mind, start exploring the surprising but real interactions between sex and money.

2. In your own mind, start exploring the interaction between sex and faith.

3. In your own mind, start exploring the interactions between sex and family.

4. In your own mind, start exploring the interactions between sex and friendship.

5. In your own mind, start exploring the interactions between sex and fitness.

Changes and Not-So-Changes, Let There Be . . .

Language is powerful. Part of the message of God creating the world through speech in the book of Genesis when He said "Let there be . . ." is that *words* can create *reality*. They shape the way we understand and relate to our world.

With this in mind, we spoke in the book about some of the changes in language in the modern world. Dogs and pets have become people's "fur babies." "Friends" are no longer people with whom we share a meaningful and close relationship, but people we are loosely associated with online. "Spousal abuse" includes abuse that takes place in unmarried relationships.

There are many more subtle and egregious examples of language changes that we did not mention. Some changes are general, and some are specific to certain fields. When one of our daughters was in third grade, her teacher sent home notes boasting about the SSR the children were doing. Like the other parents, we had no idea what SSR was. Upon asking, we parents were told that it meant "Sustained Silent Reading," in other words—reading to oneself. Of the students in that class, 95% loved reading and had to have books pried from their hands at bedtime. Using the term SSR instead of saying "reading to oneself" made the activity seem like one that only a trained professional could manage. We parents quickly realized that this particular teacher knew lots of jargon but had very few skills and little knowledge. Her language attempted to mask her inadequacy.

Exercise 6.1

What language changes can you note from when you were growing up until now? If nothing comes to mind, the next time you read a newspaper or magazine article, actively look for updated language. We'll start you off with number 1.

1. _____ Spouse has been replaced with "significant other."

2. _____

3. _____

4. _____

5. _____

Be aware of your own use of language. Make a deliberate decision as to whether you are going to adopt new language or double down on what may seem to be outdated terms.

Ironically, as changes that flow from modern mindsets seep into the system, with masculinity being labeled as toxic and women receiving preferential treatment and support as they pursue education and job opportunities, it is not clear whether people are any better off or whether the fundamentals of human society have really changed.

Exercise 6.2

1. In what ways are society and people better off than they were in 1960?

2. In what ways are men better off than they were in 1960?

3. In what ways are women better off than they were in 1960?

4. In questions 3 and 4, did you distinguish between married and single people?

5. Are you happier than someone of your age and sex was a generation ago?

6. Do you think an adolescent of your sex is happier now than a generation ago?

There were many predictions as to how life was going to change as feminist ideals became embedded in the culture. As many men would take their wives last names as the other way around. Women would propose to men as often as the reverse. Very few pundits suggested the marriage rate would radically decrease.

Exercise 6.3

Most of us socialize with people who share similar values with us. Expanding beyond your inner circle to work associates, neighbors, storekeepers, etc., do you know examples of the following? More or fewer than the reverse?

	Yes or no	More or fewer than the reverse?
1. Married couples where the woman rather than the man proposed?		
2. Men or women who have never been married and are over the age of 30?		
3. Couples (married or not) where the woman is taller than the man?		
4. Couples where the wife outearns her husband?		
5. Couples married more than 15 years where the wife outearns her husband?		

If you are not married and would like to be, or are married but are dissatisfied, ask yourself if trying to live your life according to "new" ideas is hampering your happiness in some ways. Don't just look at today, but picture yourself 5, 10, and 20 years from now and think about the consequences of today's actions. The next exercise is designed to help you do just that.

 **Exercise 6.4**

Look at the following messages about men, women, and family that we encounter in society today. In the right column, we listed some of the consequences of these beliefs. Can you fill out consequences for the others?

Belief	Possible Consequences
Having kids is something I'll do later in my life, if at all.	I'm 37 and ready to have kids. I'm discovering that fertility declines rapidly after a woman's late 20s.
Women should be able to dress however they want and expect to be treated with respect.	
Women can do everything men can do, and they can do it just as well.	
Sex doesn't have to mean anything. It is just a casual encounter.	
Getting married is something I'll do later in my life, after I have fun with a variety of people.	
Men and women should both be able to "have it all."	
Men and women don't need any help from the opposite sex. It makes absolutely no difference if they form a long-term committed relationship or not.	
Men don't need to marry. Life can be just as fulfilling and successful with a string of relationships.	
Having a family is expensive and will make me poorer.	

Sex: Pleasure and Pain

Reflections

What additional ways can you think of in which current contemporary attitudes clash with reality as you have come to see it or as biblical tradition teaches?

Can you suggest why these beliefs have come into vogue? What is the underlying message behind encouraging people to shun relationships, devalue marriage and children, and deny differences between men and women?

How would you counter the widely held but false idea that almost every aspect of human nature can be changed by law and custom? Can you express a difference between a materialistic and a spiritual worldview?

Are Men and Women the Same?

A mistaken notion of equity has taken hold of our society. Rather than helping us value men and women for their separate strengths and capabilities, we have come to expect men and women to be *the same* and to operate in similar proportions and in similar roles throughout society.

The nature of male-female relationships has always depended on which of two conflicting and incompatible blueprints is followed. The first view is that other than superficial and largely irrelevant differences, men and woman are basically the same and are indeed largely interchangeable. The second view is that male-female differences are profound and extend way beyond the biological. Furthermore, these very differences are indeed essential for the smooth running of families and societies.

Exercise 6.5

1. How might it be possible to reconcile these two views?

2. Consider how a society or a country might evolve differently over several generations depending on which of these two views was consistently followed.

3. Think of two reasons for believing that the first view could be correct and two reasons for why the second view could be correct.

Most of us observe several differences between male and female behavior. We are going to list a number of activities that tend to attract more of one sex than the other. Obviously, none of these activities appeal to 100% of one sex or repel or bore 100% of the other. Nonetheless, it belies reality to pretend that men and women are equally represented at football games.

We invite you to explore whether you believe these differences are somehow innate or whether you believe that they are due to social conditioning. You might find it fun and interesting to compare your answers with that of your spouse or a close friend.

Sex: Pleasure and Pain

Exercise 6.6

Activity	Likely Innate	Likely Due to Social Conditioning
Enjoying a football game		
Crying when returning to work after having a baby		
Going to the bathroom with a friend		
Viewing a dripping faucet as a personal challenge		
Reading romance novels		
Viewing pornography		
Wrestling (for children)		
Cuddling a doll (for children)		

The Holistic You: Workbook

Reflections

Though every person will typically possess a blend of masculine and feminine traits, in a normal distribution of population an overwhelming majority of people who produce sperm will demonstrate stronger masculine characteristics while similarly, most people who produce eggs will demonstrate a stronger predominance of feminine characteristics. A person's sex exerts an almost inescapable influence on his or her life.

When men and women have the economic and social freedom to choose their own hours of work, more women opt for part-time hours.

Exercise 6.7

Given the choice of column A or B for professionals serving you, which would you prefer:

Profession	Female with 1,000 hours of experience	Male with 2,000 hours of experience	Not relevant	Other gender-related factors that enter into my decision
Plumber				
Surgeon				
Trial lawyer				
Accountant				
Sales clerk				
Childcare worker				
Dentist				
Kindergar-ten teacher				
Pilot				
Gynecologist				
Pediatrician				

The Explosive Power of Sex

Because of the desirable and exciting polarity between men and women, they are drawn to one another. They recognize that they need each other, which creates a magnetism that we call sexual tension.

Thus we understand that the solution to sexual tension is not to get rid of it, but to contain it. Instead of trying to eliminate it by making men and women more alike, we harness it. How do we do that? Through the institution of marriage. Leo Tolstoy wrote:

> *Here is my opinion. Women are the chief stumbling-blocks to a man's career. It is difficult to love a woman and do anything else. To achieve it and to love in comfort and unhampered, the only way is to marry! How am I to put to you what I think? And Serpukhovskoy, who was fond of similes, went on: "Wait a bit! Wait a bit! . . . Yes, if you had to carry a load and use your hands at the same time, it would be possible only if the load were strapped on your back: and this is marriage. I found out that when I married, I suddenly had my hands free. But if you drag that load without marriage, your hands are so full that you can do nothing else. Look at Mazankov, at Krupov! They have ruined their careers because of women!"*[1]

Exercise 6.8

Complete if not married:

1. What needs, either physical or emotional, do you currently have that might be satisfied through a committed marriage relationship?

_____

_____

_____

2. How would having these needs met change what you are able to achieve?

3. When you see married couples, what do you most envy about their relationship.

4. What do you most cherish about not being married?

5. If you are a man, ignoring the physical relationship, how do you think having a wife differs from having a best buddy?

6. If you are a woman, ignoring the physical relationship, how do you think having a husband differs from having a best girlfriend?

_____

_____

_____

Complete if you are married:

1. Do you relate to the experience described in Tolstoy's quote of having your hands "free" after getting married? Yes/No

2. If you answered yes, describe the ways that you felt marriage "set you free."

3. If you answered no, what steps should you take to stop your marriage feeling like a burden?

4. Do you feel that both spouses should share all household chores equally?

5. If you and your spouse disagree on the answer to question 4, how might you resolve the matter?

6. Do you ever belittle your spouse for acting "just like a man" or "just like a woman"?

_____

_____

_____

The Physical Depicts the Spiritual

In *The Holistic You* we touch on several physical differences between men and women that reveal deep spiritual and psychological truths about masculine and feminine natures.

We also touched on the powerful idea that physical realities mirror spiritual ones and vice versa.

Therefore, one of our most accessible ways to seek wisdom is through biology itself. What messages did God engrave in the physical world that He wished for us to understand?

We touched on a few in *The Holistic You*. The baculum, for instance, is an appendage that guarantees reproductive performance in most male mammals. Yet human males lack it. We suggested the reason for this is that human sexual interaction is not purely a practical matter of procreation. By not guaranteeing a man's sexual performance, God's design determined that it also be a reflection of his desire and, ideally, his love for his wife.

The possession of a hymen, almost unique to human women, is an indication of the importance of exclusivity in a woman's relationship with her man. The very practical reason for this is that if a woman's loyalty is in doubt, the paternity of her child will be uncertain. For a man to be confident that his children are his own, his wife's exclusivity cannot be in question. Fatherhood, as a power for good in life, depends on female exclusivity.

But these are certainly not the only differences between men and women. To enumerate them all would be an exhausting exercise. Here are a few; feel free to add your own.

Exercise 6.9

Take a moment to reflect on some of these physical differences between men and women. Can you guess what the spiritual differences that mirror these physical differences might be?

Men	Women
Physically stronger.	Physically more vulnerable.
Body is straight, without curves.	Body is curved and rounded.
Genitals are external.	Genitals are internal.
Produce an ongoing almost limitless supply of semen that can be used to seed new life at any time.	Ovulation takes place only once a month; once pregnant, must focus on growing that one baby and cannot gestate additional children.
Beauty is not central to his appearance.	Beauty is central to her appearance.
Do not have breasts that produce milk.	Have breasts that produce milk to feed a new baby.

Sex: Pleasure and Pain

Reflections

Masculine energy is linked to ambition and aggressiveness. Men are inspired by visions of the infinite and by expansive dreams. Do you think this is a reflection of his potentially limitless amount of sperm?

The female body receives the potential hidden within the sperm and converts it to actual. The woman's body changes the possible into a living baby. Though male potential may seem immense, without the feminine power to bring it into the world, none of that seed would ever turn into a child.

Note

1. Leo Tolstoy, *Anna Karenina*, Book 1, Part 3, Chapter 21.

Chapter 7

Some Tough Decisions

Is Family crucial to a good life?

We know that a certain level of Fitness is. After all, if a person is physically ill or disabled, it is harder to enjoy and partake in life. We know that Finance is necessary for putting a roof over our heads and keeping the fridge stocked, in addition to the satisfaction that we get from serving others to earn our pay. We have explored Faith and its surprising centrality. We appreciate that Friendship, in some form, is truly integral to a healthy life.

But how does Family tie in? Our course we all have *some* family in the world, whether we are close with those people or not. We all have parents. And our parents have parents, and so on. Many of us have siblings and cousins and aunts and uncles.

But our 5Fs are based on the assumption that after one moves beyond childhood, Family implies marriage and children. It does not merely refer to the family that we come from, but to the marriage we form and the family that we build.

Yet much of modern society creates confusion in the area of marriage. It often paints marriage or having children in a negative light. Many today will say, "I have wonderful friends; they are all the family I need," or "I am close with my nieces and nephews. I don't need children of my own."

What are we to think?

Exercise 7.1

Identify three examples of how the culture in which you live beams a message that devalues marriage and family.

_____

_____

_____

_____

_____

_____

_____

_____

_____

Are Marriage and Children Disposable?

For centuries, people assumed that growing up included marriage and children. Not everyone married, but marriage was never dethroned as the ideal because it could not be achieved by everyone. No one questioned its intrinsic value to both individuals and society.

Today, many people are making the choice not to get married. They might argue that marriage is a patriarchal institution or that with longer lifespans it is unrealistic to tie yourself to one mate. Many see it vaguely in their future but not as something to pursue when they are young.

Both many singles as well as married couples are increasingly choosing not to have children. Some claim not to have the temperament to raise children. Others claim that they don't want to bring children into a world that is troubled and dangerous. Some people argue that there are too many people on earth and more will only cause more damage to a precarious planet. Others simply don't want to deal with the burden. And indeed, when marriages are weak or nonexistent, having children becomes a far more challenging endeavor.

As we have already seen, whenever one of the 5Fs is lacking or weak, it will inevitably affect the others. It should come as no surprise that in a world in which Faith is declining, Family is taking a huge hit. We may be discovering that Faith and Family need each other to succeed.

Exercise 7.2

1. How does having a strong family impact the other 4Fs?

   a. Finance: _____

   b. Faith: _____

   c. Fitness: _____

   d. Friendship: _____

2. Can you list some of the ways that Faith might complement creating a strong marriage and raising children?

   _____

   _____

   _____

   _____

   _____

3. What is the impact on society when educated and affluent people choose not to get married and have children or when the majority of children are being raised by only one parent?

   _____

   _____

   _____

4. Do you know of any successful, long-term marriages? What qualities do these marriages share?

   _____

_____

_____

_____

_____

5. What qualities, habits, and behaviors could you cultivate in yourself so that you can bring them into your present or a future marriage?

_____

_____

_____

_____

Finance and Marriage

Getting married and having children should both be deliberate decisions. Yet, our culture encourages us to rationalize why neither of those activities are necessary or why they should be deferred. Yet, as we get older, both of these choices become more difficult and sometimes impossible to initiate.

Exercise 7.3

Read the following statements and pay attention to your reaction to them.

1. Marriage puts a brake on personal fulfillment.

2. I need to be more mature before I can get married.

3. I will get married when I find the right one.

4. Raising a child costs a tremendous amount of money.

5. I shouldn't have children if I can't afford extras and sending them to college.

6. Marriage unnecessarily imposes legal formalities on an emotional relationship.

7. If I get married, I have a 50/50 chance of getting divorced.

Platonic Relationships

We have known several little boys and girls whose best friend is of the opposite sex. We've watched them play happily together, and always, sometime after they turn seven or eight or thereabouts, the friendship dies a natural death. It's always a little plaintive to watch, but somehow, they each realize that they'd rather be playing with someone of their own sex. That realization is an early intuitive sense of the power of sexual difference.

We have also watched a busy working wife enroll her husband and four-year-old daughter in a weekly "Mommy and Me" program in which he was the only man amongst a bevy of young moms. The group also would do occasional activities together such as hikes to nearby waterfalls, enjoying one another's company while introducing their toddlers to the beauties of nature. We don't think we need tell you how this story ended. Two broken marriages and a reshuffling of children.

So-called platonic friendships between men and women seem a natural benefit that sophisticated urbanites can enjoy while smirking at the less enlightened who view such relationships with skepticism and often with alarm. Due to no more than cultural conditioning and social mores, it is possible that your thinking on this topic is questionable. The following exercise is designed to help you possibly reboot your attitude.

Exercise 7.4

1. Are you or have you ever been involved in a platonic relationship with someone of the opposite sex?

Yes/No

2. How do or did this/these friendships differ from friendships you have with people of the same sex?

Yes/No

3. Have you ever been hurt or confused when either you or your friend wanted to move the platonic friendship into a different sphere?

Yes/No

4. If you are a woman, were you ever surprised to find yourself jealous when your platonic male friend started a romantic relationship with a woman?

5. If you are a man, have you ever fantasized or had sexual thoughts about your platonic female friend?

Yes/No

6. If you are married, do you want your spouse to have close friendships with people of the opposite sex?

Yes/No

7. Have you ever been involved in a platonic friendship that evolved into a romantic or sexual one?

Reflections

Many people intuitively realize the value of placing a protective fence around one's marriage. We mentioned our friendship with the late Zig Ziglar, who traveled frequently and made a point of never being alone with another woman.

"I made it clear that I was not doing anything but honoring my wife," he said. He did not say that he did not trust himself to behave honorably or that his wife jealously demanded that he make this policy. Acting as he did was a way of honoring his wife, his marriage vows, and of acknowledging the reality of sexual force.

We invite you to consider what might be some valuable fences to place in your own life, given the kind of involvement that you typically have with other men or women in business or social settings. Even if you are single, you do not want to find yourself damaging someone else's marriage.

Exercise 7.5

What are three possible practices that you might adopt to avoid getting into potentially harmful situations?

1. _____

_____

_____

2. _____

_____

_____

3. _____

_____

_____

It is hard to go against the flow. Most of us don't want to be seen as "holier than thou" or as condemning other people's choices. It is helpful to decide in advance how you will decline going out for dinner with a coworker on a business trip or how you will avoid getting involved in personal conversations.

Write out a few sentences that you are comfortable delivering:

_____

_____

_____

You may even want to practice saying them aloud.

Exercise 7.6

On a scale of 1–10 with 1 being not at all and 10 being absolutely, do you agree or disagree with the following statements? If you are female, statements 1–5 apply to you. If you are male, statements 6–10 apply to you.

Statement	1 = not at all; 10 = absolutely
1. Only an insecure man wants to earn more than his wife.	
2. In a family with children, it is irrelevant which parent is more actively involved in childrearing.	
3. I would prefer to work part time and be home part time, especially once I have children.	
4. My career is vital to my sense of self and happiness.	
5. Being a wife and mother can be a fulfilling life-choice.	
6. I expect my wife to provide at least half of our family's income.	
7. Spending a great deal of time with his or her father is as crucial to a newborn's well-being as is being with his or her mother.	
8. My career is vital to my sense of self and happiness.	
9. If I won the lottery, I would still want to earn money.	
10. I would like my wife to see being a wife and a mother as her main occupation.	

Teams Are Made of People Fulfilling Different Roles

Though completely impossible in real life, imagine how unutterably frustrating it would be to live with your clone. Although it would certainly be friction-free to live with someone who always wanted to do exactly what you wanted to do, living with someone who interrupted you with "I know how this joke ends" whenever you launched into a humorous anecdote, or who came up with exactly the same ideas as you whenever you wished to brainstorm would ultimately doom the relationship.

On the other hand, while living or working with another autonomous human being can be incredibly rewarding and gratifyingly effective, it too comes with its own difficulties and frustrations. The trick is to benefit from the collaboration while minimizing the friction.

Fear is a complicated part of being human because while it seems to serve a positive purpose in discouraging us from close association with things that can harm us, it also can deter us from scary actions that would ultimately benefit us.

For instance, a small child might have a healthy fear of barking dogs or of steep drops. An adult might avoid dangerous districts out of fear of criminal assault or desist from illegal activities for fear of arrest and trial. That's all well and good, but that same child's natural development might be delayed by ongoing fear. She might not learn to distinguish between bristling dogs and friendly puppies, fearing both indiscriminately. Likewise, fear keeps some adults from the convenience of air travel, and for the same reason, some grownups eschew professional promotion out of a form of fear.

Write down two ways that fear can be a positive emotion for an adult.

1. _____

2. _____

Write down two ways that fear can be a negative emotion for an adult.

1. _____

2. _____

Unless we can get a grip on our human ability to feel fear, it is probable that opportunities both social and professional, that is to say both in the Friendship and in the Finance arenas, will elude us. Do you think that our fear mechanism should be modulated? Should we ensure that our fear mechanism is in place to alert us of real danger but not set so high as to stop us doing things we ought to do? Give the reasons for your answer.

Yes _____

No _____

The correct answer is no. For small children, who lack cognitive development, fear keeps them safe, but for adults, fear is always a negative and indulgent emotion that is best kept at bay. Yes, we should prudently avoid dangerous districts, but not out of heart-pounding fear, but by a rational thought process that evaluates risk and reward. Of course we should avoid running afoul of the social contract we call the law by criminal behavior, but not out of panic at the thought of prison, but out of calm commitment to our internal value system and a deliberate decision to be upright.

One might choose to fly commercial but not with a private pilot in a single engine small airplane. Again, it should be the result of a thoughtful risk-reward calculation, not out of blind fear of flying. One can be filled with legitimate trepidation about a forthcoming career advancement and one can then carefully devise strategies to dispense with the concerns. That is legitimate and entirely different from feeling paralyzed by fear.

Aren't we supposed to fear God? How about the verse in Leviticus 19:3, "A man should fear his father and mother. . ."? Without going into detail, the word fear is a mistranslation of the Hebrew. A more accurate translation would be "in awe of."

Following are a number of words. Decide if each best describes fear, courage, or both.

Place each word on its appropriate line.

Indulgent. Uplifting. Challenging. Contagious. Empowering. Stimulating. Repressive. Addictive. Inspiring. Easy.

A: Fear _____

B: Courage _____

Get rid of fear and its baleful effect on your life by banishing fearful thoughts as soon as they enter your mind. Many other thoughts also need to be banished from mind. The more banishing of destructive and damaging thoughts that we do, the better we become at it.

Here are two examples of thoughts that need to be banished routinely:

1. Fantasies that do not involve your spouse
2. Burning envy of another person

Write down three other thoughts that you will work on clearing out of your mind the minute they raise their heads.

1. _____

2. _____

3. _____

We have already looked at fears caused by cultural or political conditioning. Those fears like, say, climate change, errant meteorites, or running out of space to dispose of garbage, for most people are not visceral. They don't send cold shivers of fear up your spine. They are more cerebral. Now let's glance at corporeal fears, the sort of fears that are so real one can almost taste the fear.

Fear of being beaten, losing one's job, public humiliation, becoming homeless, public speaking, losing loved ones, sexual dysfunction, physical violence, loneliness, illness, not making my partner happy, poverty.

Think about each of the above possible fears. If you had a large group of men and women, do you think they would rank the listed fears similarly? If not, place each fear on the line of the gender that thinks about it more strongly.

Men more strongly fear _____

Women more strongly fear _____

Both sexes equally fear _____

Exercise 7.8

1. Think of a successful collaboration in which you've participated. It could be a work project, planning a vacation trip, or something as simple as setting a table together with someone else. What made the collaboration effective?

_____

_____

_____

2. Have you ever had the frustrating experience of trying to do a job with someone else, but the other person kept doing your work for you? Why do you think this happens?

_____

_____

_____

3. Have you ever been frustrated when collaborating with another person because their ideas and ways of working are so different from yours, yet the final project came out better than had you worked alone? What would help you embrace such a collaboration in the first place?

_____

_____

_____

The Holistic You: Workbook

Reflections

All successful collaboration is built around some kind of division of labor. Though it's true that at various points, it may be necessary for different team members to repeat or review one another's work, a successful joint project places boundaries around the roles of each member.

If you are involved in a project and have just completed an assigned task, it is immensely frustrating to discover that your manager or another colleague completed the same task as you and rendered your work unnecessary. Collaboration without delineated roles easily descends into frustration for its members.

Yet society encourages us to treat marriage and family life as a partnership of "sames" rather than recognizing the different strengths, often based on sex, that husbands and wives contribute to create a unified, functional system.

Creating a quality life for ourselves and for a future generation should be seen as a "project." Serious projects are best accomplished by teams who bring different strengths to the table. The team that works on this type of project is the partnership of marriage.

Deliberate Decisions

 Exercise 7.9

Which of each of the following pair of statements are you more frequently exposed to?

A. A famous couple getting divorced

B. A famous couple happily celebrating their 40th anniversary

A. Encouragement to pursue a career

B. Encouragement to get married and have children

A. Disappointment in devoting a life to building a family

B. Disappointment in devoting a life to building a career

A. Fears of poverty

B. Fears of loneliness

A. Advice to play around before getting married

B. Advice to be a virgin at your wedding

A. Books, articles, and movies that stress honor and duty

B. Books, articles, and movies that stress self-fulfillment and fun

A. An optimistic view of the future

B. A pessimistic view of the future

A. If I have children, I will want to raise them to live an honorable life.

B. If I have children, I will want to raise them to be happy.

Chapter 8

Putting the 5Fs to Work

Our goal with this book was not to provide readers with an exhaustive accounting of all the ways that the 5Fs of Faith, Family, Fitness, Finance, and Friendship interact and intersect in our lives. Such a work would have been impossible!

Rather, our goal was to introduce you to a new way of thinking. In this way of thinking, we appreciate that we must not compartmentalize our lives. We appreciate that a healthy, happy life requires a holistic way of thinking. We need to integrate all five of our pillars in measured and deliberate ways.

We hope that after reading this book and working your way through the thought-provoking exercises, you will perceive many of the ways that the 5Fs interact in your own life.

How to Grow

You may be asking yourself, *now what?* What can I do? How can I change my life? And indeed, if you have read the book *The Holistic You* and completed the activities in this workbook, you may have already noticed changes in your behavior and thinking.

Where to from here?

First, acknowledge that change is difficult. All beginnings are hard, every change is a new beginning, and it helps to be forewarned. Making dramatic changes often backfires, with us dropping our resolutions as quickly as we picked them up. While sometimes dramatic steps are needed, in most areas small and easy changes done consistently are preferable.

Here are a few:

1. Address one area at a time, while keeping the remaining 4Fs on your radar screen.

2. Having taken a small step forward in one area, take a small step forward in another pillar. Repeat.

3. Make growth pleasurable. If you know you want to incorporate a new practice into your life, make it as doable and appealing in possible. Whether it is exercising with a friend, finding a budget calculator that is user-friendly, or rewarding yourself for leaving your phone far away from the dinner table, we all do more of what we enjoy. Making your growth activity enjoyable will significantly improve your chances of repeating it. The more you repeat it, the more natural the activity becomes. Be patient; change does happen.

Takeaways from *The Holistic You*

Before we introduce the final exercise, reflect on your takeaways from *The Holistic You* and from this guide.

Exercise 8.1

What changes have you noticed in your mindset from before you worked through this material until now?

_____

_____

_____

_____

Can you identify key ideas about each of the five pillars that you would like to integrate into your life?

1. Faith: _____

_____

2. Fitness: _____

_____

3. Friendship: _____

_____

4. Finance: _____

_____

5. Family: _____

_____

Exercise 8.2

In Chapter 8 of *The Holistic You,* we provided real-life examples where the 5Fs sometimes clash against each other. Just as in a marriage, things go better when you think in terms of yourselves as a couple winning an argument rather than husband or wife winning and the other losing. It helps to keep a perspective of the 5Fs winning rather than one area winning while another area loses. Long-term perspective is vital here.

You may agree or disagree with the answers we gave. In this exercise, we present you with a question pertaining to our answer that we hope is thought-provoking. Discussing the original questions and answers as well as these additional ideas with friends and family may help you understand each other better and become more adept at seeing another point of view.

Ask the Rabbi and Susan #1:

Most of us tend to fall on one side of a divide—harder on ourselves than on others, or harder on others than on ourselves. What do you believe is your tendency? Or are you hard on both or easy on both? (The brave souls among you can ask your nearest and dearest what they think your tendency is.)

Ask the Rabbi and Susan #2:

In our answer, we mentioned that there are potential problems when the husband is the boss and his wife an employee versus when a wife is the boss and her husband the employee, as in the case mentioned.

What do you think some of these difficulties might be in both cases? Do you agree or disagree that the alternate choices can lead to different problems? If so, do you think these are socially constructed problems or inherent in male-female realities?

Ask the Rabbi and Susan #3:

We suggested to the designated driver that changing the way that he feels could remove the problem. Have you ever had an experience where changing the way you felt was a better solution than trying to change the behavior of an offending party?

Ask the Rabbi and Susan #4:

In the United States today more than half of law and medical school students are female. Colleges and universities likewise tilt female. Do you think that our culture discourages men from being ambitious? Are men being lured and taunted into relinquishing masculinity? Is this a factor that is affecting your life?

Ask the Rabbi and Susan #5:

Can you identify a tendency in your life that is holding you back from being more financially successful? In Phil's case, it is his love of the new. For other people, it might be difficulty in seeing a bigger picture or, conversely, trouble dealing with smaller details. It might have to do with a character trait such as impulsiveness or a default position of not wanting to rock the boat. The possibilities are endless. Explore this idea.

Ask the Rabbi and Susan #6:

Where do you believe the line between public and private displays of affection should be drawn? What do you think might be the effect on children who see excessive physical affection between their parents versus the effect on children of seeing no physical affection between their parents?

Ask the Rabbi and Susan #7:

This question dealt with one of the topics couples should discuss before marriage, namely Faith. What other questions should be discussed, ideally with some guidance from older and more experienced mentors? Try to find at least one question for each of the 5F areas.

Ask the Rabbi and Susan #8:

Justin's question touches on one of the more countercultural suggestions we made in our book, that of not being isolated with a member of the opposite sex. How do you agree or disagree with our answer to him?

Ask the Rabbi and Susan #9:

Most of us are very emotional about our children. Almost inevitably, parents will sometimes have strong differing opinions. What's the best way to deal with these difficult situations? In addition, think of other instances where being kind to a family member may actually harm him or her.

Ask the Rabbi and Susan #10:

Have you ever experienced a situation where "doing business" with friends or family threatened the relationship? Could the problem have been avoided with advance planning?

Ask the Rabbi and Susan #11:

Does graciously receiving a gift strengthen your relationship with the giver, weaken it, or leave it unaltered? What is the reason for your answer?

Ask the Rabbi and Susan #12:

Have you had a similar experience where you thought you were speaking the same language as your spouse, friend, or anyone else, only to discover that you each understood the words you were using differently? Is there anyone important in your life—or perhaps it is you—who is reluctant to probe for clarity?

Ask the Rabbi and Susan #13:

Does your workplace function with integrity, or do you feel that you are compromising your ethics? Do you feel morally upright in how you conduct business?

Ask the Rabbi and Susan #14:

Have you ever made a decision with your eye on the long term, despite the appeal of a short-term benefit? Is there an area where you wish you had made such a decision?

Ask the Rabbi and Susan #15:

What are some "good deeds" that you find easy and enjoyable? What "good deeds" do you find difficult? Has this ever caused conflict with friends or loved ones?

Exercise 8.3

We hope that we have presented some new ideas in our book and workbook. You may wish to explore some of them more deeply. Or an idea may resonate with you, but you don't feel confident about putting it in motion.

If lack of guidance or wisdom is an issue, what can you do to begin seeking more information? Write down avenues you can follow to get more clarity.

If getting started is a challenge, what effort can you take to begin motivating yourself and committing to a new path?

Write down possible steps you can take:

1. Faith: _____

2. Fitness: _____

3. Friendship: _____

4. Finance: _____

5. Family: _____

Choose three actions from your previous list with which you would like to start:

1. _____

2. _____

3. _____

_____

Thank you for joining us on this journey. We believe that it will bring you closer to the goal of having a healthier, happier, and more successful integrated life.

We wish your holistic you blessing and success.

Rabbi Daniel and Susan Lapin

Index

Boundaries:

   blurred, between pillars, 50–52, 174

   for peace and harmony, 49

   to protect marriage, 157–158

Breastfeeding, 94

Business:

   collaboration in, *see* Collaboration

   inefficiencies in, 116–117

   integrity in, 174

   personal relationships in, 112

   spiritual aspects of situations in, 57

Business interactions, 69, 115–116

Business owners, 120, 121

Business relationships:

   with friends and family, 172, 174

   positive vs. negative, 113

   between spouses, 172

   strengths and weaknesses in, 114

Business teams, 12, 35, 160

Cain (Biblical figure), 39

Cancer, 79

Career, 141, 159, 166

Caring:

   for body, 92–93

   for possessions, 48

Change, difficulty with, 169–170

Childlessness, 84, 151

Children. *See also* Raising children

   connection to past for, 38

   displays of affection in front of, 173

   ensuring paternity of, 144

   function of fear for, 161–162

   lessons on value/money

       for, 123–124

   male–female friendships for, 155

   masculine and feminine energy to

       create, 146

   as necessary members of family, 149

   rationalizations for not having,

       153–154

   reading aloud to, 99

   societal messages about, 133, 134

   spiritual aspects of conflict

       between, 57

Churchill, Winston, 99

Clarity, in communication, 174

Climate change, 17

Collaboration:

   division of labor in, 164, 165

   effective, 164

   financial rewards for, 116–119

   and friction, on teams, 160

   frustration in, 164

Commitment, 175

Communication, 36, 174

Community, 4, 23, 74

Complex systems, 117

Conflicts, 172–174

Connection(s), 35–52

   behavior and, 41, 42

   Bible's teachings on, 39

   and boundaries between 5Fs,

       50–52

   for collaboration, 116

   family, 43, 44

   and feelings about other people,

       39–41

   finance-related, 112–114

   inventory of, 44–45

   investing energy in, 46

   need for, 35–36

Finance. *See also* Money
    boundaries between other pillars
        and, 50–52, 174
    connections related to, 43, 112–114
    crosslinks with, 28
    defined, 4, 23
    in 5Fs system, 11, 12
    health challenges and struggles
        with, 82
    integrating, 171
    interactions of other 5F pillars with,
        79–83, 151–153
    necessity of, 149
    rating health in area of, 24–25
    time and energy invested in activi-
        ties related to, 24–25
Financial health, 26, 175
Financial opportunities, fear about, 161
Financial partnerships, 116–119
Financial rewards, 116–117, 173
Fitness, 5, 79–105. *See also* Physical
    health
    balanced care for body, 92–93
    crosslinks with, 28
    defined, 23
    in 5Fs system, 11, 12
    food and, 94–97
    improving speaking skills, 97–99
    integrating, 171
    interactions of other 5F pillars with,
        79–83, 151–153
    interactions of sex and, 127
    necessity of, 149
    observations about, 79
    resistance and struggle to increase,
        103–105

sleep/rest and, 102–103
for soul and physical body, 87–91
stronger relationships for, 84–86
struggles with, 82
taking action to improve, 175
time and energy invested in,
    24–25
using vulgar/profane language,
    100–102
5F system, 11–31, 169–175. *See also*
    specific pillars
    ancient Jewish wisdom as basis
        for, 19
    boundaries between pillars, 50–52,
        174
    committing to, 175
    components of, 12–13
    conflicts between pillars in,
        172–174
    crosslinks in, 28
    growth in alignment with, 169–170
    as holistic system, 22–23
    integration and separation in, 49
    interactions between pillars, 3, 5,
        11, 52, 169
    links between sex and pillars, 127
    mindset changes in, 170–171
    rules for living in, 29
    strengthening pillars, 1, 26–27
    time and energy invested in pillars,
        24–25
Five Books of Moses, 47
Flying, fear of, 161, 162
Food, 90, 94–97
Foundational aspects of life, 11
Friction, 103, 160

Honesty, 122
Human interactions:
    customer service in, 115–116
    role of faith in, 69–71
Humanity, origin of, 61
Hymen, 144
Hypnosis, 87

Immorality, wealth and, 120, 122
Information, sources of, 19
Innate tendencies, 16, 137–138
Inner values, 62–63
Integrity, 40, 49, 174
Isolation:
    as cause of death, 79
    with member of opposite sex,
        157, 158, 173
    physical health and, 35

James, William, 12
Jargon, 128
Jealousy, 156
Job opportunities, for women, 129
Judaism, see Ancient Jewish wisdom

Labor, division of, 164, 165
Language:
    for describing wealth, 120–122
    related to faith, 55
    related to spirituality, 55–56
    for relationships, 127–129
    vulgar/profane, 100–102
Laughter, 90
Laws, 74–76
Leaders, faith for, 73
Leviticus (Biblical book), 162
Lifestyle choices, 15–17

Listening, 97–99
Loneliness, 84, 85. *See also* Isolation
Long-term view of decision making,
        174
Loss, 57
Love, 141, 144

Male–female relationships. *See
    also* Marriage
    in 1960 vs. now, 130–131
    platonic, 155–156
    resolving sexual tension in,
        141–144
    societal views of, 130–134
Marriage, 4, 23
    collaboration and friction in, 160
    cultural views of, 149–151
    deliberate decision making about,
        166
    developing faith muscles for, 71
    health, mental well-being, and, 79
    mindset about conflict in, 172
    personal view of, 143–144, 154
    potentially harmful situations to,
        158
    protective fence around, 157–158
    rationalizations for deferring,
        153–154
    resolving sexual tension in,
        141–144
    societal messages about, 133, 134
    societal views of, 132
    successful, 152–153
Married people, views of marriage
        by, 143
Masculine characteristics, 129, 139, 144
Masculine energy, 146

language changes in, 129
role of faith in God in, 70–71
struggle and exertion in, 103
view of marriage and children
    in, 132, 149
view of sex-related differences in,
    136
web of connections in, 35
Soul:
    believing in, 63
    benefits of struggle for, 103
    healing physical body and, 87–91
    remote control for, ix, x, xii
    reprogramming, x–xi
Speaking skills and speech, 97–100
Spending habits, 111
Spiegel, David, 79
Spiritual concepts, 56
Spiritual eating, 94–95
Spiritual factors in physical
    health, 87–89
Spirituality:
    defined, 55, 56
    language related to, 55–56
Spiritual nature of money, 109
Spiritual needs, 57–59
Spiritual part of self, 62
Spiritual sex-related differences,
    144–146
Spiritual worldview, 134
Spousal abuse, 127
Spouse:
    appreciating strengths of, 144, 165
    cultivating habits of a good, 153
    honoring, 157
    male–female friendships for, 156

as necessary member of family,
    149
role of, 159
working for your, 172
Strength(s):
    of family members, 144, 165
    physical, 7
    in work relationships, 114
Stress, 87
Strong relationships:
    behavior in, 42
    building, 84–86
    inventory of, 44–45
    investment of energy in, 46
Struggle, 103–105
Suppliers, relationships with, 112
Synergistic effects, 116
Systems, complex, 117
Systems-based thinking, 11–12
    about connections, 36
    about health challenges, 82–83
    about life, 12–13, 22

Teams, see Business teams
Technology, for connection, 112
Television, ix
Ten Commandments, 66
Thought exercises, 6
Time:
    connection in, 36–38
    investment of, 24–25
Tolstoy, Leo, 141
Trauma, emotional, 87
Trust, 40, 114
Truth, 60, 62
Tunnel vision, 3

187

Index